THE JOURNEY OF YOUR LIFETIME

Everything you experience in your life is part of your learning process. The way you are cared for as an infant, the way your parents and family interact with you, the way your friends treat you and the way you treat them, the people you love and those you hate, the choices you make about what to try and what classes to skip—all of this is part of the learning your brain is doing as you become a man.

Does this mean that every time you skip class you're doomed forever? Or that every time you make what you later see as a not-so-smart decision you are never going to amount to anything? Of course not! What this all means is that it is a great idea to see yourself as part of a journey as a boy who is learning his way through boyhood and into manhood armed with all of the courage and wonder you can muster. The challenges to Boy Up in a society that is so confused about the roles of men and women are not easy, but I hope we can learn together so it doesn't seem like a burden. Rather, it should be seen as the journey of your lifetime—because it is!

OTHER BOOKS YOU MAY ENJOY

BOYING UP

HOW TO BE BRAVE, BOLD AND BRILLIANT

BOYING UP

HOW TO BE BRAVE, BOLD AND BRILLIANT

Mayim Bialik, PhD

PENGUIN BOOKS

PENGUIN BOOKS
An imprint of Penguin Random House LLC, New York

First published in the United States of America by Philomel Books,
an imprint of Penguin Random House LLC, 2018
Published by Penguin Books, an imprint of Penguin Random House LLC, 2019

LIBRARY OF CONGRESS CATALOGING-IN-PUBLICATION DATA IS AVAILABLE UPON REQUEST.
Penguin Books ISBN 9780525515999

Printed in the United States of America.

10 9 8 7 6 5 4 3 2 1

Edited by Jill Santopolo.
Design by Ellice M. Lee.
Text set in Perpetua.

For my beloved sons,

MILES ROOSEVELT AND FREDERICK HESCHEL:

You are the inspiration for and

the higher significance of all of the fruits of my labor.

Thank you for teaching me about Boying Up

and motivating me to be better

at being your mama every day.

I love you more than sushi.

 CONTENTS

• INTRODUCTION •

In case you don't know already, I'm not a boy. Never was, never will be. I'm a woman who was once a girl. And then I "Girled Up"—I went from a girl to a young woman to a grown-up woman who is a neuroscientist and a mom.

I became a neuroscientist because I love everything about the brain and nervous system. My specific field of study for my PhD was a field called psychoneuroendocrinology. That's a fancy word for studying the behavior that comes from understanding how the chemicals of the brain make girls girls and make boys boys. I also studied a lot about the behavior of men and women and how the chemicals in our bodies change the way we interact with the people we encounter in our lives. For 7 years of graduate school, that's what I lived and breathed.

All of that learning happened while I made the huge decision to become a mom, and I had my first son in graduate school. Miles is now 12, and his brother, Frederick, who is 9, was born right after I completed my doctoral studies. Yup, they call me Dr. Mom when I get too technical about anything from a scraped knee to a hurt feeling to answering "But Mom, why do I have to shower? I showered three days ago!" My sons' voices, experiences and desires are constantly with me as a mom and a doctor of neuroscience; my goal is to best convey what we have learned together to all of you reading this book.

I was an at-home mom with my sons for the first years of their lives, and I returned to my childhood career of acting when my younger son was about 2 years old. Since then, I have played Dr. Amy Farrah Fowler on *The Big Bang Theory*. I love my job, and I also love being a mom to my boys. I especially love being a mom who is a scientist.

When I wrote my book *Girling Up*, I specifically talked about my journey from "girl who didn't always fit in" to "woman who doesn't always fit in," and a lot of me not fitting in is because I have always tended to gravitate toward things I was told were "for guys." You see, I'm a rough-and-tumble kind of mom, and that suits me and my sons just fine. I'm the kind of woman who is really into sports cars. I love any sport you can name; I'll watch it on TV, I'll play it, I'll talk about it—I am a sports person through and through. I am the first to suggest a wrestling match at the park. I prefer the natural history museum and building with LEGO to shopping or manicures. I love any superhero or action movie. I'm what they used to call a "tomboy," but now I just call it being me!

After writing *Girling Up*, it seemed natural to me to follow it up with the book you are holding in your hands. *Boying Up* is about the journey boys take from being boys finding their way in the world to becoming young men who can be confident, productive and loving fathers, teachers, doctors, friends, co-workers and world changers. I have included the voices of real grown-up boys—men from a variety of backgrounds, professions and lifestyles—who contribute throughout the book with "That's What He Said . . ." boxes in every chapter. I want this book to be authentic and approachable; fun and informative; diverse and meaningful.

We will cover all of the important stuff about being a boy, such as, how does the male body develop and function? What does it mean to understand how a male body grows nutritionally, physically, emotionally and even spiritually? What things do boys and young men in the 21st century need to contribute to a culture that so often misunderstands them? And perhaps most importantly, with all of the conflicting information about how boys should behave—don't be too rough, don't be too gentle—how can we together understand the biology and psychology of the process of Boying Up in a way that adds to all of our acceptance for all of the different kinds of boys that there are?

Boying Up is written for boys, young men, men who were once boys and anyone who wants to better know about the magnificent mystery that is all things boy.

Let's learn all there is to know about Boying Up together! Ready? Set? Let's go!

ONE

• HOW BOY BODIES WORK •

Welcome to *Boying Up*! You might be thinking: *why is a woman writing this book?* Well, I spent 12 years total in college and graduate school studying the brain and body, and I specialized in learning all about the chemicals in our brains and bodies that determine many important things: everything from if you develop a penis or not to what hormones make you grow hair on your body to more complicated things like what kind of emotional reactions you have and what you like to do or to wear or to watch on TV.

There is an awesome body of research about what makes all kinds of boys and men. Are you the kind of guy who likes musicals? Or would you rather poke your own eye out with a toothpick than sit through *Hamilton*? Are you someone who is interested in girls and spends time checking out which girl from your school liked your picture on Instagram, or are you someone who's interested more in other boys? Or maybe you are more interested in Nerf gun fights and video games and would rather not deal with thinking about dating at all. Do you fear physical challenges like obstacle courses, potential fights in the schoolyard and any sport involving a ball? There are so many different kinds of boys and that's what makes being human so cool: everyone is different and special.

Becoming brave, bold and brilliant is a process that begins when you're a boy and continues to get refined for the rest of your life. There are many opportunities for boys in this culture, but also many challenges, and the best way to start understanding how to navigate them is from the bottom up. Let's talk biology.

From Boy to Boying Up

Have you noticed that some girls in your class are all of a sudden a lot taller than they used to be? And that many girls in your class are

taller than most of the boys? Maybe you haven't noticed, but trust me: you will soon. This is because of an incredible process called puberty, which is the biological explanation for how you go from being a boy to a young man to a grown-up man. So why are girls taller than a lot of boys in middle school? Well, girls tend to start puberty earlier than boys (age 10 versus 12), and one of the earliest indicators that puberty is starting is a change in height. Boys tend to catch up pretty quickly, and by the age of 16, most boys are taller than most girls (though of course, this isn't true for every single girl and every single boy).

So what exactly goes on in puberty? Well, somewhere between the ages of 12 to 16 (though for some boys it might happen a little earlier or a little later), your body and brain start to change; this is a physical and chemical process, and it's a significant part of what I am calling Boying Up. Boys start to have more mature facial features and more muscular bodies, and voices deepen. The penis and testicles mature as the body prepares for the process of becoming a young man. Genitals and underarms grow hair, and these places often develop a strong scent. You will start to sprout fine hair above your upper lip, and eventually it will become thicker and it will need to be shaved unless you want a mustache. Acne or pimples may start to show up as part of puberty, and emotions may start to feel a lot bigger than they ever did before.

For some boys, these changes happen fast, but for others, they can take a lot longer. There is no "right" time to start seeing these changes; it's kind of a waiting game. I remember there were some boys in my junior high who had voices that were higher than mine even in 9th grade, but they eventually caught up.

So how does puberty actually happen?

XY

How? Well, the answer is actually Y—no, not "why" like the question; Y as in chromosomes. You see, inside every cell in our whole body, we have DNA. DNA is a bunch of molecules that are packed really tightly together and contain all of the information that our body needs to exist. Everyone's DNA is a combination of the mom's DNA and the dad's DNA, and it has information coded in things called genes. DNA contains tens of thousands of genes, which determine physical things about us such as eye color, height and whether or not we can curl the top joint of our thumbs back when making a thumbs-up. (Can you? I can!) Our DNA also has genes that determine more complicated things, such as if we're the kind of person who likes to cuddle with puppy dogs or if we tend to be confident or shy.

So inside each and every cell, there's a tightly packed ball of all of the information that determines pretty much everything about you. When a mom's egg cell met a dad's sperm cell and a baby started growing, the mom and dad DNA combined—half of hers and half of his—and it was at that very second right when the egg and sperm met that it was determined whether each of us would be a boy or a girl. The fact that you're male is coded into your DNA.

So what's the Y business? Well, the parts of our DNA that determine if we become a boy or a girl kind of look like an X and a Y if you look at the DNA under a microscope. Here's a picture of X and Y chromosomes, which is the fancy word for the structure of DNA when it gets all smushed up so that it can fit inside of every cell.

How this all breaks down is the mom's egg cell contributes an X when her egg meets the dad's sperm. A dad's sperm cell can pass on either an X or a Y; it's basically like flipping a coin, a 50 percent chance either way. So every time a mom cell and a dad cell meet, the mom gives an X to the new baby and the dad gives either an X or a Y.

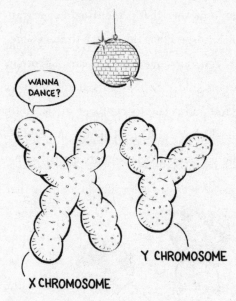

WANNA DANCE?

Y CHROMOSOME

X CHROMOSOME

If the dad gives an X chromosome, the baby ends up with two X chromosomes and develops into a female. If the dad gives a Y chromosome, the baby ends up with one X chromosome (from the mom) and one Y chromosome and develops into a male due to a critical gene called SRY, which stands for "sex-determining region Y"—not a very exciting name, I know. And not to make things weird, but the "default" of your anatomy is to develop into a girl . . . so once the Y chromosome gets added to the mix, and once SRY sends out the special "You're a boy!" message, it starts making a protein called TDF, or testis-determining factor. This means that the female body parts, which had been the "default," are told to change gears and start turning into male body parts. It's really an amazing process.

So what do Xs and Ys have to do with how we actually start puberty? Well, the X and Y chromosomes contain chemical messages on the surface of their structure that get activated at certain points in life. And the Y chromosome has the ability to start sending signals to your brain through messengers in the form of proteins and chemicals. Our brain gets told, "Yo! We're starting puberty here!" and the pituitary gland and related structures in the brain begin to release very special chemicals throughout our bodies. These chemicals are called hormones. Hormones are actually what

make us start puberty and they are responsible for all of the changes that happen throughout the process of Boying Up and beyond.

Puberty

Puberty changes some parts of your body that you can see and some parts you can't. In fact, scientists are still trying to fully understand how hormones affect our bodies and our brains.

Most people have questions about puberty. I know I did. Here are some questions about puberty you may have.

- When will my body hair start to grow?
- What's up with shaving a mustache? How does that work?
- I'm used to my body; what will it be like for my penis and testicles to change?
- Should I know about what happens to girls' bodies during puberty?
- I know boys can't get pregnant, but what should I know about the process?
- Why do I feel kind of funny when I see someone I have a crush on?

Let's get started by learning what happens similarly during puberty for boys and for girls. Both boys and girls will start to get hair under their arms, although boys tend to end up with more underarm hair than girls in general. Boys start growing hair around the penis, and girls start growing it around the vagina. Boys and girls both have a growth spurt at puberty, but, like I said before, boys' growth spurts tend to happen later, which means girls are generally taller than you for a few awkward years at middle school dances!

One change that happens to boys, which doesn't happen for girls, is that boys' voices start to get deeper and the "voice box," which is known as an "Adam's apple," gets more prominent. Other physical changes for boys include muscle mass increases, which leads to a broadening of the shoulders and an increase in muscle as opposed to fat in the chest and stomach. Jawlines and necks become bulkier and more, well, manly. This is due to a special hormone called testosterone, which boys have a lot more of than girls do.

Testosterone

Testosterone is a powerful messenger produced in your testicles by specialized cells called Leydig cells. Leydig cells send out messages to the hypothalamus and pituitary gland in the middle of your brain to communicate information about hormone levels, and this system is highly regulated and very complicated and seriously stupendous.

Leydig cells get supercharged during puberty to send out more testosterone, which travels throughout your brain and body to start the process of turning you from a boy into a man. Testosterone is secreted all of the time at higher levels once you start puberty, and it is responsible for what is called your sex drive, among other things. Testosterone levels go up and down throughout your adult life depending on environmental factors such as dating patterns and psychological stress. At around 40, testosterone

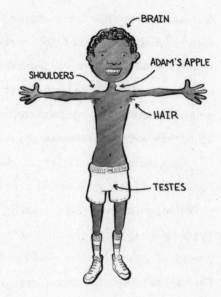

levels start to drop, taking with them hair follicles on your head that are very sensitive to testosterone. These hair follicles happen to be distributed in the shape of an "M" if you look from above— this is why many men start to lose their hair in a characteristic M shape! It's actually known as male pattern baldness.

Men produce about 20 times as much testosterone as women

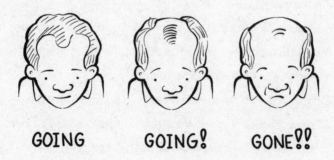

GOING   GOING!   GONE!!

do, and testosterone helps increase muscle mass and strength, which is why men tend to be stronger and more muscle-y than women. Testosterone protects men's bones and keeps them strong, and it is also responsible for many of the features boys will start to develop in puberty: a square, "strong" jawline, a more prominent brow ridge and a broader nose.

Testosterone also makes the larynx grow bigger, which is responsible for the deepness of your voice. Men's vocal cords tend to be longer than women's naturally, leading to a generally deeper voice for men than women after puberty is done. However, the process of your voice changing can take a few years to complete. During that time, you may experience some very awkward—and possibly amusing—cracks of your voice at important times in your life. Every Bar Mitzvah celebration I went to when I was 13 featured a 13-year-old boy croaking his way through a three-page speech. I promise, by the time you are in high school, most of this awkwardness should be over!

THAT'S WHAT HE SAID . . .

"I basically refused to talk until I could craft my version of what a deep voice should be. I had a best friend with an early 'deep voice,' and I would mimic it as best as I could to avoid the inevitable cracking. Honestly, a voice crack midsentence is like having the curtain pulled down while you're soaping up in the shower!"

Genetic Variations in Testosterone and Identity

Girls and women have testosterone too, but in smaller amounts. In women, testosterone is typically converted by a chemical process into estrogen, which is what causes the changes of puberty for girls. However, there are some genetic cases where a woman will be born with SRY present, and this leads to a lot of changes that we typically only see in men. Women with SRY may have deeper voices, broader shoulders, stronger jawlines and more aggressive athletic ability and sexual drive. Sometimes men are born with less testosterone than is typical, and this also affects their brain and body. Some people born with these genetic conditions undergo hormonal therapy and sometimes surgery to feel more comfortable in their bodies.

Hair

One of the more noticeable things testosterone does to you during puberty is that it adds hair to your body. Typically you'll see hair under your arms, around your penis and testicles, on your upper lip (a mustache typically grows for a while before you can try to grow a beard!) and on your chest. Your leg and arm hair may get thicker and darker, too. The order this all happens in can vary, and some boys place more importance on seeing pubic hair first, while others may want mustache hair to come in. Some boys may not feel ready for any of it, and that's not an unusual way to feel about all of these changes.

Genetics determines if your hair comes in curly or straight and if it will be dark or light. It's not always a simple science: dark-haired men and redheads typically have body hair and facial hair that is the same color as the hair on their heads. Blond men tend to have lighter-colored body hair, but sometimes they'll have red facial hair because, once in a while, nature likes to mix things up. Some men grow beards with many colors (one of my friends has a beard with black, brown, red, blond and a little gray!). The length your facial hair grows is also determined by genetics: some guys may want to sport a fancy mustache that twists at the ends, and some guys may hope to grow a long bushy beard; whether you can or can't really depends on your genes! And in case you're wondering: chest hair, pubic hair and facial hair (not leg hair) will all eventually start to turn gray when your genetics determine that they will.

While it is generally accepted that men don't shave their legs and underarms and women do, for almost all of human history, women did not shave their bodies and neither did men. Hair exists to protect vulnerable parts of your body, and it actually is made to "hold" chemical scents called pheromones, which mammals produce in order to hormonally communicate with others. In many cultures, shaving, deodorants and perfumes mask these scents, but what you do about your natural odor is totally your decision. There is quite a bit of variation in terms of what people smell like and how much odor they even have! (Also, just so you know, having underarm hair doesn't actually make you sweat more. It can make you smell more, since underarm odor comes from bacteria that lives on hair and in the clothing that touches your underarms rather than from the hair itself.)

It usually takes until your early 20s to have your hair patterns settle in. Some men will eventually grow a lot of chest hair; others may not have much at all. Not having body hair doesn't mean you aren't manly or don't have enough testosterone, and being super hairy doesn't make you more of a man than a guy with no chest hair. While there are certain conditions where men don't produce enough testosterone, for the most part, where and how your hair grows is just genetics. In most of your lifetimes (and mine!), we have seen a lot of male models and celebrities flaunting very little chest hair because they choose to trim it with clippers, shave it with a razor or remove it by going to a salon where they apply hot wax and pull the hair out from the roots. Some men—and women—prefer these grooming techniques because they think it is more clean looking. However, when I was growing up, chest hair was seen as a sign of maturity, and many guys wanted to have chest hair like a lot of the actors and musicians who were popular at that time. While some advertising companies present hairless men as the ideal, it's not true that all people prefer men to not have body hair. Body hair is natural and normal however it is on your body, and while you may make choices about trimming, shaving or waxing body hair, you are not more manly if you have tons of hair or more attractive if you don't. In fact, we are seeing a lot of men sporting mustaches and beards in popular culture in the past few years.

Some men will grow hair on their backs—sometimes in small amounts; sometimes pretty much the whole back! Many men choose to shave their back hair or go to a salon and have it waxed off. This hurts a bit while it's being done, but the results last longer than shaving. I, for one, don't think there is any need for men to shave or wax their backs or any part of their body, but some women disagree with me, and many men do. Other men like to shave (or not) because they find having facial hair (or not having it) more comfortable. It's totally up to you.

Genetics also determines when and how you will lose your hair. There are many factors influencing how and when you'll lose your hair. And thanks to a more accepting culture, men with thinner hair—and even bald men—are experiencing a lot of positive attention lately. Losing your hair is not the end of your attractiveness!

Shaving How-To from a Grown-Up Boy

As someone who has never grown a mustache or a beard—and hopes never to grow one either!—I recruited a grown-up boy to help talk about what you should know about shaving. Here are some guidelines.

Blades: Many men shave with a razor, which is typically made to be thrown out when the blade wears out (also known as a disposable razor). There are some fancy old-fashioned kinds of razors where the handle is wood or metal and the idea is to keep the handle and replace the blade when it gets dull.

Electric: Some men prefer an electric razor, which has to be plugged in or charged. Historically, blades gave a closer shave than electric razors, but new electric models are super fancy and can give a very close shave. If you want the closest shave possible, though, an old-fashioned razor is the way to go!

Skin sensitivity: A razor blade may feel gentler on your skin than an electric razor, but everyone's skin is different. If you get a rash, cut yourself frequently (these nicks usually clot within a minute or so) or your skin feels raw after shaving, try another razor or switch to electric.

Lotions and potions: If you shave with a blade, you will need shaving cream or soap to soften the skin and keep the blade from cutting you. With an electric razor, you don't need any shaving cream. Aftershave is something men used to use to help heal the skin from tiny nicks or cuts that can occur during shaving, and it is often alcohol based. Nowadays, with razors being so advanced, aftershave is sometimes just something that smells good! Keep in mind that the more you use aftershave or cologne, the more you get used to the smell, and sometimes you'll end up using so much that you can be smelled from a mile away! Always use scents sparingly to avoid kids at school calling you a skunk! Another warning: When aftershave hits your skin, you may feel a slight sting for a minute or two!

Wet or dry: Some men like to shave in the shower because the hot water and steam open up the pores and make it easier to get a close shave, since the blade is cutting closer to the base of the hair shaft. Other guys shave in front of a mirror and use the sink to rinse off their razor between passes with the blade. It's totally up to you.

Style: If you want to grow your facial hair into a mustache, goatee or beard, shave off everything that isn't where you want it like a good sculptor. And be patient: remember that young hair is softer and finer than the facial hair you will eventually have once puberty is over and your testosterone levels are more elevated.

Up or down: There are two schools of thought on which direction to shave in. Some men prefer to shave against the grain of their facial hair, from their chin up toward their cheek. This gets you a closer shave but might irritate your skin. Other men choose to shave with the grain of their facial hair, from the top of their beard line down to their chin. This is easier on your skin, but you'll end up with more stubble. You can experiment and see what works best for you!

MOUSTACHE   GOATEE   BEARD

THAT'S WHAT HE SAID . . .

"Growing facial hair is a rite of passage, and it's one of the surest ways to show the world that you are indeed becoming a man—it grants you instant bragging rights as a dude. This also means that the glorious burden of shaving will soon become part of your daily routine!"

Your Body

Let's move on to understanding your anatomy. Here's a basic map of your body.

You have a penis with a long tube inside it called the urethra, which leads from the kidneys—where urine is made—to the opening of your penis. Your penis is basically the passageway from the inside of your body to the outside. (Girls have a urethra as well, but they also have a second opening called the vagina. More on this later!) Boys' genitals—the penis and testicles—are on the outside of the body. Testicles come in a pair, and they are in a sensitive pouch called the scrotum. If you've ever been hit in the testicles,

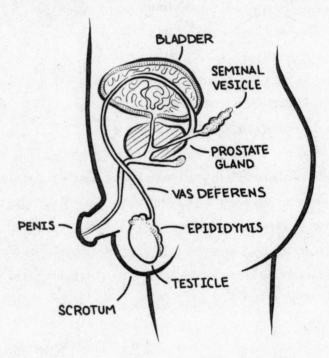

you know that it is very painful! It can be so painful that it might even make you throw up. Interestingly, the nerves that control pain from your testicles end up in your stomach, so that when you get hit in this very delicate part of you, the message your brain gets is to clutch your stomach and roll into a ball to protect your testicles from potential further damage. This instinct is primal and is based on your desire to protect your future children, because your sperm cells, which will be needed if you one day want to have children, are inside of the testicles.

The penis is a muscle, and as with any muscle, when blood flows into it, it gets activated. Because of the blood inside it, the penis can change size and become hard. That's called an erection. One of the things testosterone does during puberty is it causes boys to have erections more frequently. Especially in your tween and teen years, as your body and brain figure things out, you may sometimes have an erection at times you don't expect to. As you mature, your brain gets a better handle on when the time is really right to have an erection. So keep in mind that even though it can be uncomfortable or embarrassing, it's completely normal and it happens to every guy you know—even adults. Also, know that waking up with an erection is very common for boys and men of all ages, since the hormones responsible for erections peak at night and increase until dawn.

Penises can vary quite a bit, and so can scrotums. Ask any pediatrician, and they will tell you that some penises are longer than others; some are shorter. Some are straight, others curve a bit. Some men have the foreskin removed as babies in a procedure called circumcision; this makes the head of the penis look different from an uncircumcised penis, which has a foreskin that retracts. And even the scrotum has variability, so don't worry if you notice differences even between you and your sibling. Every body is different, and there is not really a "normal" size, shape or type of penis or scrotum!

Here are a few sketches of what some penises and scrotums look like (and all are normal except the last one!):

Emotions play a part in how your penis works, too. It's not just about blood flow at different times of the day. Part of the brain's

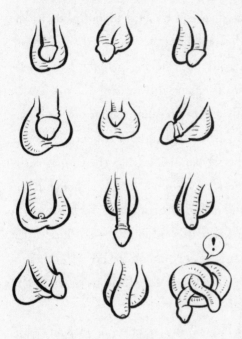

way of preparing you for becoming a young man and eventually a grown-up man is introducing chemicals in puberty that are connected to your ability to make babies. (I know you're not ready to be a dad right now, but your brain and body basically start to practice during puberty.) What this means is that your brain starts looking at

people differently to figure out who you find attractive, and sometimes when you *are* attracted to something about someone, it sends a message to your penis to fill with blood. Basically, your brain is telling your body, "Hey, that's the kind of person we could reproduce with." That whole process—looking at someone you find attractive and getting an erection in response—is called arousal.

Getting aroused and having an erection sometimes leads to ejaculation, when the penis releases sperm. The sperm are carried to the outside of the penis in a fluid called semen. Releasing sperm in semen is a normal part of being a boy and a man, and since semen contains the cells that could make a baby, ejaculating is kind of your body's way of learning how to eventually make a baby. Every ejaculation contains about 100 million sperm—they are super tiny!—and the total amount you ejaculate is actually only about a teaspoon. Semen can be white or yellow or even a light gray. While semen is kind of thick when it leaves your body, within about 20 minutes, it liquefies because there are enzymes in your semen that start breaking down the proteins.

Many boys touch their penis, and it feels good because it's nature's way of encouraging you to be familiar with a very pleasurable part of your body and your experience as a human male. While some cultures and religions have strong opinions about touching your penis, masturbation is a normal and biologically healthy thing to do. If you have concerns or questions about it, talking to someone you trust is the best way to understand it better.

The Other 50 Percent of the Population

What are some of the things you should know about girls? Don't roll your eyes or skip this section if you think girls are lame; it's important to read so you can be a well-rounded, educated male. Let's put on our scientist hat and learn a bit about girls.

The first thing many boys may think is fascinating or hilarious or weird or awesome about the female body is the presence of breasts. Breasts are fat deposits that women get over the pectoral muscles. All mammals have them but human breasts are very pronounced compared to other mammals'. Let's chat about the word *breasts* for a minute. Some girls and boys call them boobs, or tits, or melons, or knockers, or jugs, or nunga-nungas, or dozens of other rather silly names; I prefer to just call them breasts. (You may want to make sure girls are cool with you using nicknames for their body parts in general; just a tip. And other people should probably check with you before calling your penis a willy or a Lincoln log or a trouser snake, too!)

Some girls develop breasts early and get a lot of attention from boys because of it, and other girls are late bloomers. When girls' bodies change has no impact on what they end up looking like as adults; I was a super late bloomer and ended up looking like most women I know in the body department. So don't judge a girl by how she looks at 10 or 12 or even 16! Breasts actually vary a lot, even though the images of breasts we tend to see in the media show a certain shape and size that's generally thought of as "normal." Some breasts are round; others aren't as round. Some seem to stand up, while others hang down more. And nipples are sometimes a bit different too—even for boys; some nipples "tuck in," and that's nothing to worry about.

Here are a few sketches of different kinds of breasts. Keep in mind: all of these are normal!

• • •

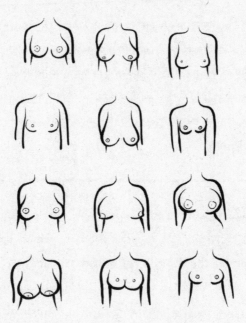

The Fascination with Breasts

There's a lot of talk in our culture about breasts, and a lot
of attention is paid to which girls or women have the biggest
breasts. Sometimes boys—and some girls—may find themselves
staring at a woman's breasts instead of her face. Boys tend to
be fascinated with breasts because breasts are sexual organs in
addition to being the things mammals use to feed babies. For
all of mammalian history, your brains have been wired to see
breasts as things that represent and stimulate arousal. Breasts
are sensitive to touch, and they are a very accessible part of
girls' sexual bodies because they are just right there in plain

27

view. Big breasts get more notice because they are easier to spot. The simple science is that it's normal for many boys to get a really good feeling in their body when they see breasts. Once you become a man, you'll see that there is a lot of variation regarding what kinds of breasts—and other body parts—you find attractive.

Let's take a glance at the *inside* of the female body.

As you can see, unlike boys' bodies, which have the penis and testicles on the outside, girls have all of their reproductive

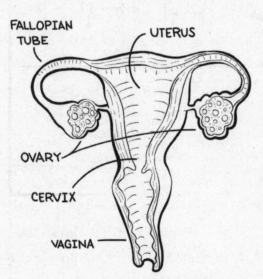

organs on the inside. Instead of testicles in a scrotum, girls have a set of ovaries, one on each side of their body right near their hip bones. Remember we talked about the genes on your Y chromosome that make girl parts into boy parts? Well, your testes started out as ovaries. Yup. Each ovary is about the size of an almond, and they are where the egg cells needed to make a baby are stored.

The Testes Journey

Once ovaries start becoming testes in a developing baby boy, they begin to make their way to the outside of the body so they can find their eventual place in the scrotum. In the process of the testes making their way to the outside of the body, there is sometimes a weakening of the path they take, leading to about 4 percent of baby boys being born with what's called an inguinal hernia, or a slight rupture in the muscle wall of the groin, which allows the intestines to poke out a bit. This normally resolves on its own, but sometimes there is a minor surgery performed to repair the rupture. Girls can also get inguinal hernias, but it's much more common in boys. Another amazing thing about the testes journey is that in about 4 percent of babies, one (and less commonly, both) testicles don't make their way all the way down into the scrotum! By the time a baby is 9 months old, the testicle has usually "dropped" on its own. If it hasn't, this can be repaired with a minor surgery.

All you see from the outside of the female body is what is called the vagina, and that's NOT what girls pee out of. Girls pee out of a urethra just like boys do. Their urethra leads from the kidneys to a separate opening, which is really close to where the vagina is. The vagina is a passageway that leads to a very significant and amazing part of the female body called the uterus. The uterus is where the baby grows, and when it is time for a baby to be born, it moves down from the uterus and comes out of the vagina.

The way girls' bodies get affected by the hormones of puberty is the ovaries start releasing and sending out egg cells from the ovaries through a sort of corridor called the fallopian tubes. Then the egg hangs out in the uterus. An egg cell in the uterus can meet with a sperm cell and become a baby, but it can also make its way out of the body unfertilized in a process called menstruation. Girls usually call this "having their period."

A lot of boys and sometimes even girls feel weirded out talking about periods. But there is nothing to feel weird about. It's normal, it's biology, and it's how we all got here. When I mention it, my sons avoid talking about it as much as possible, but I don't want them to be afraid of knowing about biology. And I don't want them to be weirded out by girls. It's important to not only know about your body but also to know about the bodies of females, trust me.

I'm going to break this down and tell you only the things you really need to know about menstruation, and I'll make it very brief. I'll even use bullet points so you know I won't elaborate much! Here we go:

- A period comes about once a month and usually lasts 5 to 7 days.
- An egg cell is super teeny tiny, like smaller than the dot on this letter *i*, but when it comes out, it comes

out with the lining of the uterus, which means there
is blood.

- There isn't a lot of blood, but it has to be
"contained," and girls typically use menstrual pads
or tampons.
- During a period, girls and women sometimes feel
achy, crampy or cranky. This is normal—it's due to
all of the hormones making menstruation happen!
- It's not cool to tease girls about having their period
or say it's gross or make up weird names for it; just
chill out and let nature do its thing!

Behavior

The hormones that get activated to make all of the changes happen
during puberty don't just affect our bodies; they also alter our
behavior. During puberty, boys and girls start acting differently and
taking interest in things in a different way. You might start caring
more about how you look, wondering about dating and thinking
more about your body—and it's all because of your hormones. The
puberty hormones are getting you ready to be a grown-up and
eventually a parent, if you choose to be a dad.

Have you ever heard people talk about how different boys and
girls are? Well, during puberty they become even more different in
many cases. Boys have a certain set of DNA in every cell of their

bodies, which contains genetic information and messengers. A boy's DNA is programmed to make you generally behave in certain ways. And girls have a different set of DNA that makes them generally behave in certain other ways. You may have heard the word *masculine* used to describe traditionally male behaviors and *feminine* used to describe traditionally female behaviors. These don't always apply to every boy or girl you know, but I'm sure you can think of examples from your own life of masculine and feminine behaviors and characteristics. Here are some common stereotypes that we often hear about boys and girls, which relate to masculine and feminine qualities.

MASCULINE	FEMININE
Boys like cars and wrestling and superhero movies and making jokes about farts and burps.	Girls like to dress up and put on makeup and do their nails and think about boys.
Boys aren't good communicators.	Girls spend a ton of time talking on the phone and texting their friends and looking at social media.
Boys like rough sports.	Girls don't like playing rough or even getting dirty.
Boys are unemotional.	Girls are super emotional.

Do any of these descriptions sound wrong, or do they not match someone you know? For example, do you know any boys who like to dress up and are kind of emotional? I do. Do you know any girls who love cars and sports and superhero movies? I'm sure you do. (I was that type of girl, and I'm that type of woman!) There are certain things about boys and girls that are true a lot of the time in all different parts of the world. For example, the stereotype that girls talk more than boys is pretty much true everywhere in the world. But does that mean that every single girl talks more than every single boy? Of course not. It just means that in general, certain things about girls and boys are true.

Even though our DNA determines whether we have a penis or a vagina, and even though our DNA generally guides how we behave, there is a lot of variation in how people act, and that doesn't mean there is something wrong with them. There are boys who are masculine and boys who are not very masculine. And there are girls who are feminine and girls who are not as feminine. And that's okay.

A lot of times, boys who are not masculine and girls who are not feminine get teased for being different. This can be really painful for them. It is important to understand that there are all different kinds of people and there is nothing wrong with being different. There are some places in the world where people accept only two genders as possible identifications. In other places, people can be described as male, female, or another category of gender that has qualities of both masculine and feminine. Some cultures even have several different ways they describe people's gender, and descriptions of more than two genders have been recorded for thousands of years.

Countries around the world with cultures that recognize more than two genders.

There has been a lot of discussion in the United States in the past few years about people who feel that even though their DNA says that they are male, they don't feel male, or if their DNA says that they are female, they don't feel female. Some people who feel that way want their external appearance to match their internal feelings. Other people don't. There's not a right or a wrong answer to what to do in that situation.

What is important to acknowledge is that not everybody's body works the same as anyone else's, and no one can know what is going on in someone else's brain and heart. There has been some really neat scientific research looking at the hormone levels in the brains and bodies of people who say they feel like they don't match their DNA. Research indicates that there are true hormonal differences, and my hope is that we can find a way for all people to feel welcome living however they feel the most comfortable.

Wrapping Up

We've talked about some big stuff in this chapter. We talked about how puberty takes you from being a boy to a young man to eventually becoming a full-on grown-up man. You may have a parent who's cool with talking to you about the changes in your body and how they affect you, but a lot of times, it can be hard to talk about this stuff with your parents or even with your older siblings or friends. Keep in mind that most boys your age and even a little older don't always have accurate information about these kinds of things . . . so always double check with a more reliable source! And a lot of boys don't feel the need to talk this stuff through; it just kind of happens. That's fine, too.

I hope this chapter has helped answer some questions about not only your body but the bodies of the girls you know, because it's important to have that information in order to make you a better man. And sometimes the stuff kids talk about isn't scientifically accurate, and it can be confusing to not really know what's going on. Information and knowledge about everything makes for excellent Boying Up.

TWO

• HOW BOY BODIES GROW •

I wrote a book when my sons were younger with our family pediatrician about the science of nutrition and diet choices and the importance of putting a lot of thought into how we feed our bodies. Now that we've talked about how a body gets to be male and how puberty begins to turn boys into men, let's talk about what your body needs to stay strong. Even though Boying Up requires many decisions about what to wear, what music to download, and how to act on a date, what's really important is what's inside of you—and what you eat and how you treat your body matters a lot, especially as you start puberty. It's very important to understand how our bodies use the fuel we give them when we eat and drink and how that fuel turns boys into healthy men.

Drink!

Let's start with the basics. About 60 percent of the human body is made up of water. That means that all of the molecules that we are made of—oxygen, carbon, hydrogen, nitrogen, calcium and phosphorus—combine to make us mostly water! The amount of water in our bodies can change if we don't drink enough—or if we drink too much—since the body needs to be hydrated in a very special way. There are minerals called electrolytes in blood, urine and all of our body's fluids. We take them in from the foods we eat and the beverages we drink. Sodium, potassium and calcium are all electrolytes. The thing about electrolytes is that they carry an electric charge; some are positively charged, and some are negatively charged—think of them like batteries with a positive or negative end. We have to have the right amount of electrolyte charges for our bodies to function properly. Without the right balance, we can get really sick.

What this boils down to is that your body needs tons of water, and most people don't drink as much water as they should. We should aim to drink as many ounces as half of our body weight per day. So if you weigh 120 pounds, aim for 60 ounces of water, for example (that's approximately half a gallon).

Here are some of the things that can happen to you and your body if you get dehydrated because you haven't had enough water. Spoiler alert: none of them are fun.

- Dry lips and mouth
- Cracking skin
- Not sleeping well
- Feeling tired all day

- Getting sick a lot
- Having a hard time concentrating
- Muscle cramps
- Headaches
- Dizziness
- Bad breath
- Not being able to poop (!)

I'm not going to claim that I never drink soda or juice, but I try to do it very rarely and mostly for special occasions. Why limit it? Well, soda and juice taste good because they are full of sugar, and sugar tastes great. But the problem with sugar is that it kind of messes with the chemistry of the body and can make you feel cranky and jittery or sore in the stomach. Sugar is bad for teeth because it's the favorite food of the bacteria that live in your mouth. Too much sugar eventually wears away the protective enamel layer of the teeth, which leads to cavities. Too much sugar also weakens the immune system, which makes you less likely to be able to fight off things like colds or the flu. Also, sugar has addictive properties, which means that sugar gets into the cells of the body in such a way that when the body doesn't have sugar, it makes you feel like you need it. Not getting sugar when the body is addicted to it makes you feel grumpy and shaky and out of it. The more sugar you eat, the more chances you give your body to get addicted, so I recommend cutting back on sugary drinks now for your body's sake.

Water World Experiment

Drinking only water every day all day might sound awful; I know. But it might be worth trying as an experiment—even for a few weeks. Adding sliced oranges, cucumbers, or berries makes it taste more interesting than drinking it plain. And keep in mind that you need to give your body a few weeks to adjust to cutting back on sugary drinks; it takes some time for your body to lose the craving. If you do a 2-week experiment and add to your experiment cutting back on other high-sugar treats, you'll probably be impressed at the shift in your taste buds.

Eat Up!

The government recommends that meals in the United States include foods from the following categories: fruits and vegetables, protein, grains and dairy (or a nondairy source of calcium if you choose to stay away from dairy). Here are the basics of what you need to know about all of the things there are to eat.

FRUITS & VEGETABLES

Have you ever heard how important it is to eat your vegetables? Well, it is. Same for fruits. Fruits and vegetables contain vitamins and minerals such as potassium, fiber, thiamin, niacin, folate (folic acid) and vitamins A, B, C, D and K. The body takes all of these in and uses them to do things like make muscles strong, keep you healthy, keep your skin looking good and keep your brain working well so you can not only pay attention in class but also have a lot of leftover energy after school to shoot hoops, play video games and hang out with friends. Vitamins and minerals do so many things in the body, and without them, we'd really be in bad shape. So please: eat your vegetables—and your fruits!

Fruits and vegetables are especially important to eat in as natural a form as possible. Meaning: however the fruit or vegetable grows is probably the healthiest way to eat it, and if it needs cooking, the less you add to it, the better. So instead of drenching strawberries in maple syrup and covering them with powdered sugar, learn to love strawberries exactly as they are. And think about a sweet potato. The healthiest way to eat it is baked, not mixed with marshmallows and sugar and

butter and made into a sweet potato casserole—although if you're going to eat it that way, once a year on Thanksgiving is a good time to do that. With a few exceptions (such as carrots, tomatoes and eggplant, which actually increase in nutritional value when you cook them a little bit), pretty much every fruit and vegetable is healthier to eat just the way it grows or with only slight cooking and very little sauce on it.

PROTEIN

When you think of protein, you probably think of the most common way people in the United States eat protein: by eating meat. Chicken, beef, pork, lamb and fish are the most commonly known sources of protein in this country. Protein is what all of the cells are made of in every single part of the body and brain. And protein itself is made up of collections of elements such as carbon, hydrogen, oxygen and nitrogen. These elements combine to make what are called amino acids, and there are 20 of them, 9 of which the body cannot produce on its own and are called essential amino acids because they are . . . well, essential. In order for the body to support the brain, spinal cord, digestive system, kidneys and immune system properly, we need to eat things with plenty of protein to get all of those amino acids. Without the correct amount of protein, our muscles won't work, we can't even think straight, and damage to our cells can become hard to repair by the body's natural protective methods. Boys and men need more protein than girls and women since the composition of their bodies is different and the hormones that vary in men and women change the way protein is metabolized and used by the body. Even though boys and men need to consume more protein than girls and women (56 grams a day for adult men versus 46 grams a day for women), too much protein can cause health problems as well, so it's important to find out how much protein you actually need.

While in our country eating animal protein is very common, there are many healthy countries around the world where people don't get all of their protein from animals; they get it from non-animal sources such as beans, nuts and seeds. You can also find protein in things like rice and even bread and pasta. People who don't eat meat for health reasons or because they don't like the idea of animals being used for food can still get the right amount of protein.

Protein Powder

Protein powder is something that's added to foods like shakes or smoothies to increase the amount of protein you consume without you taking in as many extra calories as you would by eating foods packed with protein. Protein powders tend to be marketed to young men during puberty because they are the ones who can be most enticed by promises like "build more muscle faster!" The fact is that if you eat a well-rounded diet, you are likely already getting enough protein. In addition, too much protein can be hard

on your kidneys and can lead to dehydration in teenagers. Consulting with a doctor about your protein intake is important, especially if you like lifting weights or are looking to bulk up. Don't be swayed by the expensive and fantastical claims of the protein powder and protein drink industry!

And although there has been a trend of young people adopting a vegetarian or vegan diet as a way to lose weight (or for philosophical reasons), avoiding or limiting the animal products you consume is a lifestyle choice that should be done with care and conscious decision making; it's not a way to lose weight. Girls aren't the only ones concerned with body weight. More and more, boys are feeling the pressure to be

skinny and fit, and restricting your eating is not a solution to body image concerns. We will talk more about eating disorders later on in this chapter.

THAT'S WHAT HE SAID . . .

"I choose to be vegan, and the reason has less to do with animal rights than with general health. Healthful eating decisions are a really important thing for me, which was not always the case. I treat my body as a sanctuary. It can be socially isolating at times; it's probably harder for guys than women. And it's particularly difficult in the dating world because most of the women I date are neither vegans nor vegetarians. It can be awkward, and I also don't drink alcohol for the same reason I don't eat animal products or processed foods. I don't feel like there's a real health benefit to drinking alcohol. These things are very important to me, and I have to deal with those choices on a daily basis."

Where's the Beef?

Meat, cheese and fish are not the only ways to get protein!

Here are some of my favorite ways to get protein without using animal sources.

Beans: Ever had three-bean chili? It's one of the best ways to get a high-protein meal. Adding beans to burritos, salads and even pastas is an easy way to get plenty of protein. Beans are especially good when they're turned into spreads like hummus (which is one of my younger son's top 5 favorite foods of all time), so keep an open mind about beans.

Soy: Since there is some evidence that soy isn't good when eaten in large amounts, soy products should be eaten in moderation. However, tofu (made of mildly processed soy beans) is a great protein source. Processed soy is available in ground form for use in tacos and burritos, and there are many ways soy beans make for great protein sources such as veggie burgers and even nondairy cheese slices.

Nuts: You might like peanut butter (I sure do!), but have you ever tried almond butter? It's just as tasty and has more "good" fats (the monounsaturated kind) and less of the "bad" fats (the saturated kind). Learning to love snacking on raw almonds, walnuts and cashews is a terrific way to get protein and also healthy fats. A handful of almonds and an apple is one of my favorite snacks.

Other choices: Grains like oats and quinoa, which is actually a seed, have a ton of protein.

CARBOHYDRATES

Carbohydrates are the main source of energy for our bodies. "Carbs," as they are often called, are important because they are built of sugar. I know we just talked about how a lot of sugar isn't good for us, but the right kinds of sugar—such as those found in healthy carb-heavy foods—are very important for giving our bodies and brains energy. Whether you are going to run a mile in gym class or cram for an algebra test, your body needs carbs to get your muscles moving efficiently and your brain thinking clearly. Have you ever heard anyone say that breakfast is the most important meal of the day? That's because overnight, when you aren't eating or drinking anything, the level of sugars in your body drops, and in the morning, eating carbohydrates helps jump-start the brain and the body. Carbohydrates generally come from starchy foods like rice, oats, bread and pasta. They can also be found in certain fruits and vegetables such as bananas, broccoli, carrots, apples and potatoes.

Sometimes we hear people saying that they want to "cut back on carbs" and that carbohydrates are bad for us. It actually turns out that carbohydrates themselves are good for us, but the way we eat them tends to be with a lot of sauce and often a lot of added artificial sugar and fat. So for example, pasta can be a great healthy meal that provides a lot of long-term energy (runners tend to eat pasta before they race in a big marathon!), but if you throw a ton of cheese and butter on the pasta, it can actually make your energy decrease. And if you don't move your body enough, carbs don't get burned off, which can contribute to weight gain. Foods made with whole grains, like whole-wheat bread and whole-wheat pasta, are broken down by the body slower, so you feel fuller for longer, meaning whole grains provide a better source of energy for your body.

Gluten is a protein found in any food made with wheat, barley or rye, which are in a lot of the most common carbohydrate products like bread and pasta. Some people—more girls than boys, interestingly—are allergic to gluten, and they don't feel well when they eat it. People with celiac disease aren't able to digest gluten at all, and it can be dangerous for them to eat even a little bit of something containing gluten. If you notice that you get gassy, bloated or constipated after eating bread or pasta, talk to your doctor about it. There are lots of gluten-free bread and pasta choices around that taste pretty close to the real thing, so don't worry if you need to limit your gluten intake.

DAIRY OR NONDAIRY CALCIUM

A small portion of the government's recommendation of what we should eat is dedicated to dairy or to a nondairy source of calcium. Dairy is high in calcium and protein, but it can also be high in fat and sugar and salt, so you want to be careful which dairy you choose to eat. For example, eating yogurt for breakfast is very different from eating a giant ice cream sundae every day as your source of dairy.

A lot of people get an upset stomach when they eat dairy because most of the population actually can't fully break down the milk protein from cow's milk. Up to 95 percent of certain groups of people such as African Americans, Asian Americans, Jewish people of Eastern European descent and Native Americans can't process dairy well at all. If you've ever noticed that you get a bad feeling in your stomach after eating pizza or ice cream, speak to your parent, doctor or even the school nurse about it. There are plenty of ways to get enough calcium if you don't eat dairy. It's in beans, tofu and a lot of vegetables too, especially leafy greens.

FATS AND OILS

We hear a lot about food products that are low fat or no fat—and based on all of the ads for weight loss programs and plastic surgery, it seems like there is something wrong with eating *any* fat. It turns out that we actually need a certain amount of the right kinds of fat in order for the body and brain to have energy to function well. Fat helps cells do the important work of dividing and growing. Fat protects the organs of our bodies and helps keep us warm when it's cold, and fat helps our bodies absorb nutrients from what we eat. Fats are needed to produce the right amounts of hormones as well. There are a lot of healthy sources of fat such as olive oil or the oils that are found in walnuts and almonds and cashews. Avocado is a great food to get healthy fat from, and it can be dressed up as guacamole or in three orders of avocado roll sushi, which my younger son has routinely been known to consume in about 15 minutes at any Japanese restaurant! Foods that contain a lot of oil or anything that's fried in oil, such as chicken fingers and onion rings, have a high concentration of unhealthy oils, and you want to try not to eat those every day (even though they are super delicious!).

Easy Guacamole

Do you know your way around the kitchen? I hope so! If not, here's a great way to start. Get 3 avocados and a knife, spoon and fork. Carefully cut the avocados all the way around and open them up. Take out the pit carefully. Scoop out the green flesh with a spoon, put it in a bowl and use the back of the fork to mash it up really well. Then, add any or all of the things below, mix it up and eat with chips, carrot or celery sticks, or on a piece of toast.

- 2 tablespoons chopped-up cilantro, raw onion or tomato
- 1 tablespoon lemon or lime juice
- 1 crushed clove of garlic
- ½ teaspoon salt

Note: if you have any guacamole left over, put a piece of plastic wrap over it and smush the wrap down on the guac so little air gets into the bowl; that's what turns that pretty green guac brown!

Food Choices

There is so much talk regarding what kind of foods we should and shouldn't be eating. People tell us all sorts of things:

Eat more fruits and veggies.

Don't drink soda.

Eat whole grains.

Don't eat too much gluten.

Eat less red meat, but make sure you get enough protein.

Don't eat too many sweets, but don't deprive yourself.

Don't eat fast food . . . But what if that's what's easiest to get? And fast food tastes really good, and it's inexpensive, so what could be better, right? The thing to know about fast food is that it's full of sugar and salt; it also tends to have a lot of fat. It's the sugar, salt and fat that say to your brain, "YUMMY! EAT ME! EAT ME!"

The problem is that fast food and other foods that are high in carbs and salt and sugar make our bodies take in a lot more calories than we necessarily should in one meal. Over time, this can cause a ton of health problems such as diabetes, high cholesterol and high blood pressure, which we can avoid if we simply don't eat a lot of these kinds of foods. I know you're thinking about the kids you know who eat a lot of fast food and still look healthy, right? Well, remember that for some bodies, health problems won't happen right away, but it absolutely will catch up with you, and it can really mess up your plans for the things you can do and enjoy. Remember: the goal here is healthy insides AND outsides!

In order to make healthier choices, some people adopt a particular way of eating that can help them make better food decisions. For example, in certain parts of the world, people believe that eating animals is unhealthy for their bodies and their spiritual selves, so they don't eat meat at all. In Japan and China, people historically live long and healthy lives, and they eat a lot of fish but very little dairy and not a lot of red meat. In most every country in the world, the main source of protein is not meat, and the U.S. has the highest rates of weight problems, cancer, diabetes and heart problems. Countries that start eating like we do here in America, by importing our processed foods and opening fast food chains, eventually start having the same kinds of health problems we have here, so there is a definite connection there.

Because of this, some people have started adopting some variation of a vegetarian diet. Vegetarians tend to eat dairy and eggs, but no meat or fish. Sometimes people will cut out meat but still eat fish, and those people are called pescatarians. People who follow a vegan diet (I'm one of them) don't eat any animal products at all. That means no meat, no fish, no dairy and no eggs. Being vegan or vegetarian is not impossible to do, but it does take a little bit of research so that you maintain your overall health. You can't just eat French fries all day and call yourself a vegan or vegetarian—you have to make sure you eat enough of a variety of healthy food to keep your body operating at its best.

Being vegetarian or vegan isn't for everyone, and that's fine. Remember this no matter how you eat: every meal is an opportunity to make good choices, and no one eats "perfectly" all of the time, so don't make it about perfection. See if you can expand your tastes and your mind enough to explore the possibility of making a commitment to your body to do the best you can for it, one meal at a time. Some people and even some schools in this country have been participating in Meatless Mondays, which is a fun way to try out eating less meat as a start.

Usually, it's our moms and dads who decide what we eat, at least when we're younger. If your parents are anything like my parents, they do not want to hear you criticizing what they're feeding you. It's okay to tell your folks that you've been learning a bit about food and nutrition and maybe there are ways you can all make some healthy changes, as long as it fits into the budget. Chances are if you bring it up as a way to make everyone's eating better, it won't be seen as a criticism. Offer to help carry groceries, shop with your mom or dad and, even better yet, offer to help cook or clean up to show you are part of the team.

One of the best ways you can make the load lighter and have a say in how you eat is also a skill that every boy and man needs to master. This will add to your Boying Up experience and contribute to making you an incredibly valuable member of the male gender: learn to navigate in the kitchen. I probably don't have to say this, but cooking and helping out in the kitchen is not just for girls. When your grandparents and maybe even some of your parents were young, that's how it was viewed, and it created generations of men dependent on women in ways that were not always healthy for the men (or, in a lot of cases, the women in the relationship). Every person will at some point need to care for themselves without a mom or dad or husband or wife doing it for them! Watch your parents or others you know in the kitchen. Watch how they wash produce, prepare meals, use a knife and other kitchen utensils and clean up. Learn to set the table, and ask questions about food prep. Some of the most famous chefs in the world are men, and even if there is no fame or fortune in your future regarding cooking, at the least you'll be self-sufficient, helpful in whatever home you live in when you leave your folks' home, and you'll be a reminder to future generations that it should be the norm to be a man who knows how to cook!

Mindfulness

One of the most important things to consider whenever we eat anything is an amazing idea called mindfulness. This is exactly what it sounds like: being mindful and taking notice of what we're doing, no matter what it is. This idea has its roots in Eastern philosophy from thousands of years ago, and it's the basis of a lot of meditation and yoga practices, but it can apply to eating, too.

In many cultures and religious traditions, people pray before or after they eat, and although this may not work for some families, the idea is a smart one because it evokes a sense of mindfulness. Eating is something that many people in this world take for granted.

Sadly, not everyone has access to the amount and kinds of foods we have access to. The next time you eat, take even a second to acknowledge that you are grateful that you have food. If you want, be specific and acknowledge that whatever you are about to eat is something you hope will nourish your body and your life. It might feel silly at first to practice mindfulness in eating, but it's actually an important thing to try to master.

Why is mindfulness important when we eat? How many times do you just start shoveling food into your mouth at mealtime? I know I'm guilty of that, and mindfulness encourages me to slow down. When we eat quickly, we tend to eat more than we should, and we often end up with an upset stomach from not giving our bodies time to catch up with digestion. Being mindful also helps us remember that eating is something we are part of, not just something that happens to us. Introducing moments of calm into whatever your mealtime looks like can help you see food as part of what keeps you going, and not something to take for granted.

Sending Messages to Your Brain

Did you know that it takes about 20 minutes for your brain to get the message that you've eaten enough to be full? When you eat, food hits your stomach, and your stomach sends signals to part of the brain called the hypothalamus, which is in charge of a bunch of things, like knowing when you're full. If you keep eating during the time it takes for the message to get to your hypothalamus, you end up continuing to eat before your brain can signal for you to stop. The way to prevent this is to slow down!

Exercise

Get some exercise! I know you probably hear this every day at school and maybe even at home, right?

Take a walk!

Find a sport!

Go run around!

Stop looking at your computer/the TV—get out of the house and move your body!

Okay, maybe that's just what my parents would shout at me, but I'm sure you know what I'm talking about. There are government programs designed to make us move our bodies and advertisements popping up everywhere reminding us to move more.

I'm not going to lie: they're all correct. Exercise and moving our bodies is something we need to do every day. For most of human history, people didn't have cars or taxis or buses or trains. Think about it: if they wanted to get somewhere, they walked (well, or maybe rode a horse). And even when people started building villages and then towns and cities, not everyone drove. People still walked a lot. Nowadays, many of us live in places where you can't really walk much of anywhere. Sure, you can walk around the block or in your immediate neighborhood, but where I live, if I want to go to the market or get to a school or go meet my friends, I have to get in the car.

There are places around the world where walking a lot and getting exercise daily is the norm. And do you know what those places have in common? The people who live there are generally healthier. Turns out, moving your body releases endorphins from your brain, which decreases your overall stress level and makes you feel calmer. People who live in places where they move a lot tend to be in great shape; they are healthier on the inside: they get sick less, they report feeling better in general, and they enjoy a life with fewer medical problems.

A lot of boys are encouraged—even more so than girls in our culture—to be active in sports and athletics. An obvious side effect of being involved in any sport is that you'll end up getting in shape, whether that's your reason for doing it or not. Whether it's running track, swimming laps or playing a team sport such as lacrosse, baseball or basketball, your body gets a great workout from being an athlete. Your body functions as a much more efficient fat-burning machine when you have a lot of muscle and less fat. Participating in a sport also puts you in touch with your body in healthy ways. You learn to make healthy choices about what foods best feed your body in order to be strong and fast, and you learn to have an appreciation for the amazing things your body can do. With team sports, you get to socialize, which can make the whole experience more fun. A culture of encouraging participation in sports and athletics also decreases the probability for putting things that are bad for your body into it, as drugs and alcohol significantly cut into your performance as an athlete and hurt your chances of keeping your body optimally healthy and fit.

What if you aren't interested in sports? Well, that's fine; not all guys are. But even still, moving your body is very important, and a lot of guys take up skateboarding or biking as a way of moving their body and getting from place to place. Walking is a great example of a healthy way to get exercise that is free to do; all you need to walk is you and some shoes that feel good on your feet. Put on some headphones and walk, even for 15 minutes a day. Walk around the block if you want to—if it's safe to do in your neighborhood. I sometimes go walking on city streets, but keep in mind, city-street walking means you get stopped by traffic lights, and sometimes people have dogs that want to sniff you, and sometimes people walk too slowly in front of you and it can mess up your groove. But sometimes it's fun to see new things as I walk, as long as big, slobbery dogs don't bug me too much!

I also like to find places that are made for walking without cars and dogs and lots of people around. There are probably places in your city or town you've never explored, so get online and find out! Searching local parks or local trails is a great start. It's going to take a little bit of effort, but it's an investment in your body and your health. Do it!

Unless you prefer being alone or zoning out to music or a podcast, walking with a friend can help you cover a lot more ground than if you walk alone. With a buddy, you can talk along the way and find ways to motivate each other. When my boys walk together, they always come up with races to do, find pinecones and tree berries to throw at each other and generally pass the time better together than they would alone.

Body Issues

Sometimes the things you experience as you transition from a boy to a young man can be intimidating or overwhelming. The changes of puberty combined with the new ways your body grows can make you feel like you don't understand your body anymore. You spend so many years having the body you call yours, and then—*BOOM!*— it changes, and it has different requirements, and clothes don't fit the same, and it can be kind of freaky, especially if puberty starts earlier for you than the other guys and if it happens faster than you expected. My older brother literally grew 6 inches in the summer before 11th grade and had to buy all new clothes and shoes in a very short period of time!

There are so many shapes and sizes of bodies, but we tend to see one kind of male body in the media: super muscle-y and thin. And pretty much all of those pictures are Photoshopped to make the men in them look more muscle-y and skinny. Seeing those images on TV and in movies and ads in magazines and on billboards

can kind of mess with your head. Sure, there are some guys who are naturally free of fat and tend to be really muscular, but a lot of men's bodies need a fair amount of weight lifting and cardio exercise to achieve muscles and look as toned as the dudes in all of those cologne and underwear ads.

When boys and men compare themselves to the Photoshopped exaggerated images they see of men in the media, it can make some of them feel like there's something wrong if they don't look like that. Pretty much everyone wants to fit in. We don't want to feel left out, and when we do feel left out, we feel bad. The smartest thing we can do to make those bad feelings less bad is to do things that make us feel good just the way we are. Surrounding ourselves with positive images of men we respect and embracing people we can look up to who support us loving ourselves is important; so is finding supportive people to talk to about feelings if we want to open up that way.

However, what a lot of people do—boys and girls both—is to try to find ways to make themselves look like those people we see images of. Many young people start dieting at a very young age, and many feel shame about their bodies at a time when the body should be celebrated and enjoyed for being able to make them run and play and learn and grow. This happens to boys and young men even though people often think it typically just happens just for girls and women.

It's healthy to want to make improvements to your appearance and your body, and if you are struggling with health problems or have spoken to a doctor about needing to make changes in your body, becoming aware of what size food portions are appropriate is a great start. Although all bodies are beautiful, being overweight can prevent you from doing sports, feeling confident, or living a life free of medical problems. Obesity can lead to conditions such as diabetes, high blood pressure and cholesterol and a host of other problems. Learning about how exercise can help burn calories and learning to practice mindfulness are also great things to do. It's important to know, however, that dieting can be very unhealthy, and it can also create a mental state of not being happy with how you look, which can grow into a bigger problem.

Note: remember that if you are *not* struggling with weight or other health issues, it is totally normal to eat a LOT of food in the years when you're transforming from a boy to a man! Your body is growing and changing and needs fuel to help it do that. Plus, it takes more calories on average to fuel a 6-foot-tall body than it does a 5-foot-tall body.

Although we usually think of girls as having a skewed perception of what they look like and having eating disorders, boys feel that way too, and it's nothing to be ashamed about. Here are a few descriptions of eating disorders boys sometimes experience. If one of these descriptions sounds like something you do, you should talk to a grown-up that you trust and see if they can get you help. You want to stay healthy as you Boy Up, and having an eating disorder prevents that.

Anorexia nervosa is thinking you have to lose weight and always feeling you are fat even when you are at a healthy weight. Anorexia nervosa is not just a way to diet; it starts with changes in your brain that get more problematic the more you restrict your eating, as the parts of your brain responsible for making decisions get confused. When people have anorexia nervosa, they often skip meals, eat very small portions or eat only very low-calorie foods. They get sick a lot, lose hair and feel cold much of the time. Sometimes people with anorexia take laxatives or diet pills so that they lose more and more weight, which can lead to intestinal problems and electrolyte imbalances, organ failure and damage to the heart.

Bulimia nervosa is an eating disorder that involves making yourself throw your food up, and people with this disorder tend to be overweight or of normal weight. Sometimes in addition to throwing up food, bulimics will deprive themselves of food for days or weeks on end but then binge, eating large amounts of food at one sitting, even when not hungry, and hiding what they're eating while also experiencing a lot of guilt. (Not throwing up food but binging and then feeling very guilty after is a separate disorder called binge-eating disorder.) Bulimia can also cause stomach acid to burn sores into your throat and mouth and eat away at your teeth.

Exercise bulimia involves eating enormous amounts of food at one time and then exercising for hours upon hours in order to lose the calories from the food eaten. This can cause weak bones and make you prone to injuries.

If you're looking for resources to help handle eating disorders, either for yourself or for someone you know, here are a few places to start:

- Go to the NEDA website, NationalEatingDisorders.org, and click on Help & Support.
- Visit the website for the National Association of Anorexia Nervosa and Associated Disorders at anad.org and click on the Get Help menu.
- Check out Eating Disorder Hope's website, EatingDisorderHope.com, and click into the Eating Disorder Treatment Centers section for resources listed by state.

Wrapping Up

The years surrounding puberty will see your body change from that of a boy to a man very quickly, and the demand on your body is great. Knowing what to eat and how to exercise so as to optimize your body's ability to grow strong and healthy is a huge part of Boying Up. Food should be enjoyable and should provide sustenance; exercise should lift your mood and provide you with a healthy outlet for aggression.

The choices you make about how you eat, including being mindful, can improve not only your health but, more importantly, your understanding of your relationship to your body. Changes to your diet and lifestyle don't have to happen overnight; the first step toward a healthy body and mind starts with awareness about what you do, an understanding that making changes takes time and a willingness to be open to making healthier choices while forgiving yourself if you don't do it perfectly all the time. Take care of your body as if it is a sacred special place. Because your body is your vessel for all of the learning, exploring, fun and adventure your life as a boy and a man will bring you. Keep it strong and healthy.

THREE

• HOW BOYS LEARN •

One of the cool things about Boying Up is that you learn all of the time. You're probably thinking, *What? It doesn't feel like I'm learning all of the time, and if I was aware of learning all of the time, I definitely wouldn't think it was cool!* Well, guess what? The brain is made for learning even when we don't think we're learning. Whenever we experience anything consciously or unconsciously, it gets stored in our brain even if we don't actively register it.

So how does information actually get stored in the brain? There is a seahorse-shaped region of the brain responsible for memory and learning called the hippocampus (*hippos* is Greek for "horse," and *kampus* is Greek for "sea monster"!). The hippocampus is made up of several layers of specialized cells, which are all bundled up like

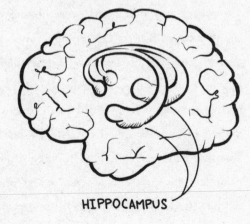

HIPPOCAMPUS

a strudel, making communication between all of the layers very fast and very efficient. When we experience something, the cells fire in specific ways to make an imprint in this region of the brain. If we need that information later on, the cells can refire and help us recall it.

Not all experiences and memories are treated equally by the brain. Memories that have emotional content—such as the fact that I can remember everything my first-ever boyfriend, Josh Netburn, said to me and even what I was wearing the day we stood in the Hebrew-school hallway outside of our 4th-grade class and he broke up with me—are stronger and easier to recall in detail. Memories associated with music or with a particular smell are also typically easier to recall, since they are made with extra information surrounding them, which adds to the strength of the memory as it is being stored, as well as increases the chance that it will be easier to recall later on.

Before we learn more about how you learn, though, let's take a step back and look at the overall basics that boys need to initiate the process of Boying Up. Being a boy is a journey you are taking part in, and this journey is well described as a journey of yourself as a hero; it's a "hero's journey," which is the expression used by many psychologists to describe this process. One such psychologist named Joseph Campbell published a book called *The Hero with a Thousand Faces* in 1949. This book became—and still is—a classic in understanding the way we organize our journey in life. In particular, the language Campbell uses applies really well to men in our culture, no matter if you're the kind of guy who likes ballroom dancing or one who likes to play video games where you can take aim at ballroom dancers (don't harm any innocent dancers in any video game, please!).

The main points of Campbell's exploration of the hero's journey are that a hero goes out into the world with a sense of wonder and greatness (known as departure). He encounters challenges that transform him (initiation), and he returns from his adventure with a sense of empowerment and is now able to empower others (return). Campbell believed that this is the path of every man, and it can be a really powerful way to understand your journey as a boy becoming a man. You will encounter a world of wonder and you will meet many challenges, but your ability to conquer those challenges and return better and stronger is what makes you you.

Everything you experience in your life is part of your learning process. The way you are cared for as an infant, the way your parents and family interact with you, the way your friends treat you and the way you treat them, the people you love and those you hate, the choices you make about what to try and what classes to skip—all of this is part of the learning your brain is doing as you become a man.

Does this mean that every time you skip class you're doomed forever? Or that every time you make what you later see as a not-so-smart decision you are never going to amount to anything? Of course not! What this all means is that it is a great idea to see yourself as part of a journey as a boy who is learning his way through boyhood and into manhood armed with all of the courage and wonder you can muster. The challenges to Boy Up in a society that is so confused about the roles of men and women is not easy, but I hope we can learn together so it doesn't seem like a burden. Rather, it should be seen as the journey of your lifetime—because it is!

This chapter is all about the ways we learn, with a special emphasis on what kinds of things boys and young men need to know to grow into grown men who are competent, respectful and awesome. We aren't just going to talk about the learning we do in school—we will talk about that, but it's not all that learning entails. Learning is also about the things programmed into your DNA that set you on a course for adventure, excitement and growth and that serve as the foundation for the man you will become.

Learning Your Basics: School

Some of us love school, while others would rather be anywhere but in a classroom! Some of us don't mind being in school because we get to hang out with our friends there, but the classes and home-work part of it feels not as much fun as the hanging out with friends part. I get that.

Why do we go to school? Most people think we go there because we have to, and I guess we sort of do. But we actually go to school to learn the things we need to know so that we can leave high school with a certain set of skills. School is preparing you for life. No matter what kind of job you decide to have in your life, you will need to have basic training in how to read, how to understand and interpret what you read and how to communicate, both in speech and in writing. A basic understanding of math is super important so that when you are a grown-up, you can manage your finances and go about life understanding how to handle and make decisions about money. That's the kind of stuff we learn in school.

Learning stuff in school may not always come easy, but the possibility exists for you to challenge yourself and work toward anything you want to be. Finding the way you learn best is a key to opening that door to the future. If you are struggling with learning, consider talking to a teacher you like, even if they don't teach the subject you're struggling in. Or speak to your school guidance counselor or advisor. See if they can help you figure out what ways you might best learn the things you are having a hard time with.

Here are some of the tips for learning success I have gathered over my years in school.

1. **Don't skip class.** It may seem like it totally doesn't need to be said, but I'm going to say it anyway: do NOT skip classes. I know you may not be able to say you'll NEVER skip class, but here's the thing: the best way to learn is to be where the learning is happening. Once we start a habit of cutting class or not valuing putting our butts in seats in a classroom, we start a pattern of falling

behind and needing to play catch-up, which makes learning hard. Consistency is key for the brain to make the most of a learning environment. Treat school as if you're getting paid to be there, as if it's your job. And if you think about it, someday, the job you have that pays your bills and buys you a house and the car you already know you want will come from the time you put in right now going to class and being in school. So get to class like your life depends on it—it kind of does!

2. **Keep an assignment notebook.** Staying organized and on top of assignments makes it easier to learn. Get a small notebook and decorate it with drawings or leave it plain; whatever you like. Every day you're in school and an assignment is handed out, make a list and write down when it's due. Even if the teacher hands it out on a printout or directs you to an online syllabus, put it in your own handwriting anyway. Writing things down makes your brain think about them and remember them in a new way. Nerdy fact about me: all through middle school and high school, I would color coordinate my assignment notebook with a different color pen for each subject. That may not be your thing, but whatever you can do to make your assignment notebook and schedule of

what's due when clear and organized will help you
a ton in getting it all done!

3. **Don't procrastinate.** Although there may
   sometimes be reasons you can't do your homework
   right away and some brains need a break before
   tackling homework after a long day at school,
   you learn best if you can practice the things your
   teachers talk about pretty soon after they talk
   about them. Doing homework close to when the
   subject matter was introduced in class means your
   brain will take the information most available and
   commit it to memory most reliably. If your brain
   works well when you take a break after school by
   running around, or if you have a lot of after school
   activities, make a set time each night that you
   buckle down on homework, and stick to it! Enlist
   the help of your mom or dad to make sure you
   keep to it.

4. **Learn to say no to distraction.** There
   will be a lot of distractions that will try to get
   between you and school and homework, and
   every distraction takes away from the brain's
   power to master something. Our brains need a
   clear and simple message when they're trying
   to learn. Text messages asking you to hang out
   rather than do homework, or even just the pinging

notifications on your phone saying that you have messages waiting to be read, get in the way of your hippocampus doing its job. Say no to distraction by turning off your phone and the TV during study time, and you'll get more done and get it done best for success later.

5. **Repeat it again and again.** And again. One of the most important factors in learning and memory is repetition. The more times we think about something or study something, the more reliably it will be stored in long-term memory. Flash cards can be used to learn just about any subject, and they can be reviewed anytime, anywhere. Making lists of things to memorize is also a great way to engage the motor system (writing) in the memory process. This makes for stronger memory formation and better learning and recall when it's time for a test.

6. **Get creative.** Don't just read to learn, engage other parts of your brain and body in the process! Writing (and rewriting) important words and facts engages your brain in ways that increase stimulation for the hippocampus and encourages it to remember all of those important details your teacher will quiz you on. Another hippocampus-stimulating trick to optimize learning is to make facts you need to memorize into songs. Introducing a musical

component to learning hits the hippocampus extra hard and makes for strong memories of things like the order of the planets, which I only remember because my 8th grade science teacher sang the order to a really catchy song with an easy-to-remember melody. Be creative, and your hippocampus will reward you!

THAT'S WHAT HE SAID . . .

"The brain is a fluid structure. It's not static. The things you repeat when you study contribute to neural circuitry maintenance and our brains' 'hard-wiring.' Because the brain is so fluid, we need repetition of not only school-work and studying, but also of our values and desired behaviors."

Learning Your Instincts: Moving, Processing, Winning

There are a lot of stereotypes about boys and girls, which we discussed in the first chapter. "Girls are more emotional than boys" is not always true. Neither is "Boys hate talking about feelings" or "Boys are athletic and girls aren't." But here's the thing: these

My Boys

My sons were raised without the influence of television and movies for many years of their childhood, which was a choice their dad and I made partly so we could let them develop their sense of being boys independent of what the media expected them to be. Much as they liked carrying around dolls and playing in their toy kitchen, they eventually naturally gravitated toward a lot of typical "boy" behaviors, and they ended up making improvised weapons from LEGO and twigs and anything they could find!

stereotypes happen to be true a lot of the time. All over the world, overwhelmingly so, boys tend to be less emotional and less verbal than girls, and boys also tend to be more physical than girls. Does this mean that there is anything wrong with a boy who is emotional and verbal and hates sports? No. Does this mean that athletic girls who don't like to talk about their feelings are weird? Nope. Does it mean that you can judge someone's love life or decide who they should want to date or marry based on whether or not they are emotional, verbal or athletic? Absolutely not!

But the purpose of understanding the process of Boying Up means understanding that there are certain aspects of boys that are generally found to be true because they are coded in the male DNA. Remember that Y chromosome you got from your dad that made you turn into a boy? Well, that Y chromosome has a ton of important protein communication signals literally on it, and they not only transform your genitalia into boy parts as opposed to girl parts; they impact the hormones and the behaviors you have in your life as a boy and a man.

So what does this mean practically? Well, you are programmed to learn by moving, exploring and being physical, particularly when there is a "winning" aspect to physicality. The stereotype of "boy" in our culture is of a kid who climbs trees, makes weapons out of twigs, builds forts and pretends to defend his fort from imaginary villains. While these are not the *only* things boys like to do, it is generally true that boys like these kinds of things. And even for boys raised without TV or movies that might "teach them" to

do these things, it tends to be true that boys all over the world like to climb and run and explore and participate in defensive-type play.

INSTINCT #1: MOVING

In hunter-gatherer societies, women raised babies in groups with other women and needed to communicate well with these other women. This made evolution select for women who were good communicators. But men were typically out for much of the day hunting and protecting territory. Boys today carry all of those genes with them for hunting and protecting even if they live in the suburbs or in a city. These genes translate in modern times into a strong desire to move and to learn by moving about and exploring.

One of the best ways our culture allows for boys to move their bodies in productive ways that help them cultivate strength, endurance, teamwork and aggression is through sports. When boys participate in sports, they learn not only how to throw or catch or run or jump, but also about setting goals and meeting expectations. They have to cope with losing and also with winning; through sports, boys can start to be sensitive and compassionate because of the interactions athletes are constantly having with others. They also master how to work well with others, taking into account their strengths, weaknesses and needs, which is one of the most important skills to have—you'll need it for the rest of your life!

It's healthy for boys to learn through their bodies, so embrace your need for movement and exploration and physical play! While my two boys tend to be very cautious when it comes to scaling fences and climbing poles and such, I love that they love to wrestle and participate in sports, and I join in when they let me. However, if you feel you *need* to move your body at times when others are still and you find it very hard or seemingly impossible to keep from fidgeting or moving around, it can cause problems in school, and it may be something you need help with. Some bodies are simply wired for movement, and young boys are not really made to sit in a classroom for 8 hours a day without wanting to move around! While for some boys, sitting for this long is not a problem, for many boys—and girls, too—this can feel really restrictive.

In recent years, we have seen a huge increase in diagnoses of ADHD (Attention Deficit Hyperactivity Disorder). ADHD is a disorder where individuals have trouble paying attention and sitting still, and they find it more difficult to control behaviors that other kids can control more easily.

What accounts for this tremendous increase in ADHD diagnoses? Some of the increase may simply be more awareness, since for a long time, we didn't know what to call it when this behavior presented itself; now that we know what the symptoms are, more people will get the diagnosis. That doesn't account for all of the increase, though. There have been numerous studies trying to isolate a genetic basis for ADHD, but some researchers have suggested that the increase in computer use, fast-paced video games and television, and even an increase in the pacing of modern life may be leading to brains wired for not sitting still or taking time to process information. We may not yet know exactly what is leading to this increase in diagnoses, but one startling statistic is that 3.2 percent of kindergarten teachers and only 19.3 percent of elementary school teachers are male. It has been suggested that female teachers may be more likely to perceive "normal" boy behaviors as problematic without more of a male presence in classrooms to balance out the diagnoses. While it may not be true that all female teachers do this, it is possible that in classrooms without enough men, the under-standing that boys are active and physical as part of their learning may not be getting the attention it needs. And with more and more emphasis on more classroom time and less outside time, many kids may feel stressed out or anxious, which can lead to being fidgety; but this is not the same thing as ADHD. For more information about ADHD diagnosis and treatment, visit www.add.org or go to www.nimh.nih.gov and, under the Health & Education tab, go to Consumer Health Publications, and click on the Attention Deficit Hyperactivity Disorder link under the Browse by Disorder head-ing. You can find a couple of helpful articles there.

Treating ADHD

Diagnoses of ADHD are usually made by specialists. With the increase in diagnoses and the lack of resources in many communities, it's becoming more common for pediatricians and counselors to label someone as having ADHD. Medications are usually prescribed when behaviors cannot be controlled by behavior modifications such as redirecting behavior, working on stress modulation and using methods of reinforcing behaviors that are desired and not reinforcing those that are not. People with ADHD may not have enough of a naturally occurring chemical in the brain called dopamine, so ADHD drugs aim to increase the amount of dopamine circulating. These drugs tend to be stimulants, which can disrupt sleep and lead to a decrease in appetite as well as increase your heart rate, and they can take several weeks to work effectively. Some nonstimulants can be used if stimulants produce adverse effects, and antidepressants, which increase dopamine and norepinephrine, are also found to be useful for some individuals with ADHD. Adverse reactions from such medications can be hard on growing bodies, so never take a medication without talking to your parent or a trusted adult first. And know that medication is not forever. Plenty of adults have ADHD diagnoses and function very well without medication after learning some basic organizational and lifestyle techniques that minimize distraction and increase focus time, productivity and a feeling of satisfaction.

INSTINCT #2: PROCESSING

Men Are from Mars, Women Are from Venus is the title of a book written by a popular psychologist named John Gray in 1992, when most of your parents were in junior high or high school. This book breaks down the differences between men and women very simply, and one of Dr. Gray's main points is that when men are upset, they often need to not talk about it. This is the exact opposite of what a lot of women need to do when they are stressed out or upset, and this can cause a lot of tension in male-female relationships.

It's important to know that you don't have to talk about your feelings if you don't want to. Sometimes the best way for men or boys to feel better is to retreat and to think about things *other than* the upsetting thing. This way of processing things is the male brain's way to protect from emotions that—generally speaking—men are not as naturally skilled at talking about. While some men do enjoy talking things out, it's totally normal to not want to engage when you are upset.

There is a difference between putting reactions on hold and pushing them down entirely. Distracting yourself with watching TV or playing video games, for example, can be very helpful, but know that, eventually, emotions do need to be dealt with, especially in a culture that encourages men to be sensitive and communicative.

Here's a helpful tip for those of you guys who may not feel like talking when people want you to: if you know you don't want to talk, say so nicely. Words can be hard to find, especially when we are upset—that's true for boys and for girls—but even saying, "I need some time to think," can be much more helpful than running away and slamming a door in someone's face. Even a little communication goes a long way. If after some time of being alone or not talking about something, you find yourself feeling genuinely better, know that others may still want to talk about it, and part of being a human is listening even if you don't feel like talking! You can also say, "I am feeling better, and I am happy to talk now." Or if you feel up to listening but not talking, you can say that, too. Like this: "I still don't feel like talking, but I can listen if you want to talk."

THAT'S WHAT HE SAID . . .

"Some people wear their emotions on their sleeves and seem to have instant access to them. For me, emotions are not always readily available. I may be hurt deep down and not really even know it. I need to be alone to process emotions because it gives me the time, the space and the sense of safety I need to come to terms with big feelings."

INSTINCT #3: WINNING

For most of human history, boys and men were out hunting and protecting territory, and this set of instincts is natural and still a part of your DNA even though we don't live in communities where boys and men need to hunt and protect like they did tens of thousands of years ago. What this means is that boys and men tend to gravitate toward activities and spending time doing things that re-create those primal DNA-programmed instincts to hunt and protect. One of the most direct ways this is satisfied is by participating in activities that involve winning.

A great example of how to satisfy this drive to win is through sports. We talked about the importance of sports for your physical and emotional development in Chapter Two, but it is also a very important thing for boys to be exposed to because of the winning feeling you get in touch with; even the desire to win gets you in touch with this very important part of yourself.

Other positive examples of getting that winning feeling can come from things like academic achievement or from nonathletic game play such as role playing games (like *Dungeons & Dragons*) or video games.

The feeling of winning in even small ways is very important for the development of boys because it establishes confidence and a notion of success, which turns them into young men who know their strengths and the feeling of accomplishment that comes with hard work and effort. These are important qualities for all people, but especially for boys who are Boying Up.

Beware of the Obsession with Winning

While winning is an important thing for boys to learn about, the desire to conquer and feel the thrill of success can become problematic if you find yourself wanting to collect conquests. If you feel unable to cope with the feeling of losing or you find your anger hard to manage when you don't win or get your way, it's a good idea to talk to a parent, school counselor or other trusted adult about it. Winning, while important, should not define you. Working hard and dealing with challenges that come up from not succeeding right away teach us a lot about ourselves, too. Tackling these kinds of feelings early on is the best way to not let them get out of control and control you.

Learning Your Culture: Media

When I was your age, I loved going to the movies, and I typically watched a few hours of television every weeknight after my homework was done. On the weekends, my brother and I would watch cartoons in the mornings while my parents got to sleep in, and once in a while, we rented a movie from the local video store to watch as a family (it was kind of like having Netflix in our neighborhood!).

My parents were pretty strict about what movies and TV shows I could watch, and there were many times when I missed out on movies and shows that my friends were watching because my parents were concerned about language, violence and nudity. Kids gave me a hard time for not being able to go to certain movies with them, and it was embarrassing. Now that I am a mom and have kids of my own, I understand what a delicate juggling act it is to be a parent and how much of our time watching movies and television is teaching us things about our culture and the world. If you have strict parents like I did, I have no magic that can make your parents change their minds. What I can say is that even if it seems like a big deal when it happens, in a few years, it won't matter at all. I hope you believe me!

What many parents know, and what we often don't get when we are not yet parents, is that all of the movies and TV shows we watch add to our learning because the things we see and experience when we watch movies and TV become a part of our brains and, in some way, make up who we are for the rest of our lives. I often tell my sons that there are certain things that exist in the world that are really intense and that, once you see them, you can't unsee them. Have you ever seen a movie or a TV show that made you feel sad and emotional but you watched it with a friend who had absolutely no reaction to it? Have you ever seen something in a movie or on TV that was really upsetting and made your stomach hurt, but

other people who saw it didn't find it upsetting at all? How about this: have you ever seen something on the news that made a friend of yours feel yucky and grossed out, but you felt totally fine about it? That's because everyone has different levels of sensitivity to different things.

Why are we different this way? Well, part of it is just genetics. Some people are super resilient, and they don't feel affected by emotional stuff much at all, while other people are more sensitive, and they feel very affected by emotional stuff. Neither of these are the right or wrong way to be. They are just different.

When boys are in the process of Boying Up, there are certain things in the media that are particularly complicated for them to learn about, that can be harmful and that, in some cases, may impact the decisions their parents make about what they can and can't watch. The categories of things that you should know about when it comes to the media you consume are—you may have guessed it—sex, drugs and rock 'n' roll—and violence.

Sex, Drugs and Rock 'n' Roll

Sex is a beautiful thing because it is the way human beings connect with other human beings. If you want to make a baby, sex is the way you do it—that's amazing! If you want to experience the wonderful, profound sensations we can have as loving, connected human beings, being intimate with someone makes that happen. (We'll talk more about this in Chapter Four!)

So why am I going to get all "Mom" on you right now? Because everything you see on TV or in the movies or even in a magazine ad or billboard on the side of the freeway contributes to what you learn about women and sex. Everything. Even if it's something you disagree with or hate, your brain saves it for later.

I am not going to be delicate with words here because it's

important just to say it: any TV shows or movies you see that show women being poorly treated or abused become part of your learning about women and men and relationships. This does not mean that you are going to behave like the poorly behaving men depicted on many shows, but what it does mean is that you are being introduced all of the time as boys to information about women and men that may not be healthy for you or for relationships in general.

The hardest thing to wrap your brain around is that there are things that seem really harmless when you see them, but they can contribute to a larger lack of understanding about women, men and sex. I can't even count how many movies I saw growing up that portrayed gay men as silly, weak and subjects for ridicule. Even movies made now tend to make a lot of jokes about gay men that become part of how we frame gay men in

How Much Screen Time Is Too Much?

After many years of research and analysis, the American Academy of Pediatrics has officially announced that screen time should be limited to under 2 hours per day. Yup: *2 hours a day.* We end up pushing aside physical activity, social interactions and schoolwork when we engage more with our screens than with the outside world. As an experiment, keep track of how many hours you spend a day on your computer or in front of the TV. Find ways to be selective about the time you spend with your screen and see if you can feel a difference in your life. You might be surprised!

our minds. And the same is true of jokes about women and girls and sexual stuff; we learn all of that when it's presented a certain way over and over. Parents often want to wait until your brain has developed a bit more before letting you see all of that, since early exposure to this kind of stuff can make your brain have expectations about what's normal, even if it's not normal or healthy.

Many movies and TV shows depict a lifestyle that you may think looks cool, but that is not healthy for your developing learning brain. Depictions of men drinking, doing drugs, visiting strip clubs and being physically abusive and violent are things we see a lot of in the media. Such activities are often depicted as the "norm," and for some men, they may be. But they're not the norm for all men, and seeing this kind of lifestyle normalized starts to work its way into your brain as acceptable. The media is powerful, and especially when we are young and see actors and musicians and sports figures we look up to engaging in behaviors we know are not so healthy, we start to try and make sense of this.

One of the best ways to combat some of the less-than-flattering portrayals of women and men and even lifestyle choices is to put yourself in situations where you can learn from seeing positivity in action. Surrounding yourself with friends and situations that seek to elevate men's and women's relationships and encourage you to strive to be all that you can be is really important—even if it sounds kind of silly. You learn by example and not just by being told to do this or not do that, so the more you see respectful communication, kindness, politeness and gentle words from men and women, the more likely you are to make those things a part of your worldview and your expectations for yourself. You may find these people to learn from in your home, or you may find them in the homes of friends or family members. You may even find some positive role models on TV and in movies, but know that the best kind of learning about social expectations and standards of being an all-around good person comes when you are watching it in action.

Learning Your Passion

Even though I was a social kid, there were a lot of times in my life when I wasn't around tons of friends. I remember times when I would tell my mom and dad I was bored, and they never liked hearing that at all! I spent a good amount of time when I was little playing outside and riding my bike, but once I hit the tween years, riding my bike just didn't have the same appeal it did when I was younger.

One of the things I started to cultivate as I entered middle school was hobbies. Now, when you think of hobbies besides sports, I bet you think of the boys in your classes collecting baseball cards or postage stamps (that's what my brother collected when we were kids!). Or maybe you think of a loner teenage girl doing puzzles by herself (that would be me!). Hobbies are interests we have that we can pursue alone, but sometimes we pursue them with others. Hobbies can involve learning a skill or a set of skills, doing crafts or playing a musical instrument. Hobbies can be playing board games, collecting comic books or learning all about a particular historical period. Hobbies use learned skills as a springboard for imagination and creativity. Your brain thrives on new stimulation as well as your ability to incorporate learned information that may seem simple, but with a little creative input, can delight and bring joy. That's the most rewarding kind of learning you can experience.

So, what are some of my hobbies? Well, I started playing the piano in kindergarten and have continued playing to this day. I learned how to play trumpet in my elementary school when I was 10, and I continued to play in orchestra and jazz band through middle school. I learned bass guitar when I was 16 and played with a few bands in my college years, although I was a very shy performer, so that didn't last long! Music is a wonderful hobby, and it is also a terrific outlet for emotional release. In addition, the brain does amazing things when mastering music. Musical ability has been linked to advanced math ability as well as increased creativity in other fields. It's never too late to learn an instrument, and I know this because I learned how to play the harp for *The Big Bang Theory* just a few years ago!

Another hobby I have is sewing and crafts. I was raised by a mom who knew how to sew really well—her parents were both tailors—and my mom passed on her love of sewing to me by teaching me the different kinds of stitches, how to assemble clothing patterns and how to make blankets and pillows for my dolls. The things my mother taught me were invaluable: she taught me using math, geometry and color theory, but she made it fun, interesting and inspiring. Some of the most memorable times I had with my mom as a child were learning with her—not just learning how to sew, but learning alongside her. That's kind of how learning works: learning things with others is its own process of learning. We learn skills, but we also learn about interaction, relationships and what we like and don't like.

As I got older, even though I didn't play with dolls anymore, my love of being crafty stayed with me.

I've dabbled in a lot of other crafty hobbies, such as painting with acrylics, making pot holders, learning calligraphy, experimenting with papier-mâché and weaving friendship bracelets. My sons and I have started trying out something called felting, where you use a felting needle to turn a ball of wool into amazing and elaborate shapes, like animals and even people.

This is the first thing my sons and I felted: a little snowman wearing earmuffs. Come on: admit that this is pretty cute!

Wrapping Up

Our brains are made for learning: how to survive, how to communicate, how to exist as humans on a very complicated planet. As boys, you have a lot to learn that helps you make the journey of a lifetime: the hero's journey. You learn to take that journey when you move your bodies, when you work hard to understand emotions and when you best understand what it means to win and what it means to lose.

Learning how to focus in school builds our brains, but so does playing sports, watching TV and doing things that bring us and others joy. We are learning beings, and we are creative beings. Good school habits, making wise choices about your free time and taking an active and engaged part in your journey to Boying Up will make you a well-rounded person and a satisfied one as well.

FOUR

• HOW BOYS LOVE •

Human beings are just one of millions of living things on the planet. We are *Homo sapiens*, a special kind of mammal that can have very complicated and meaningful relationships with other *Homo sapiens* (as well as dogs and cats and a variety of other critters we sometimes have as pets!). *Homo sapiens* have significant relationships with parents, siblings and other family members, as well as friends and romantic partners. These relationships are defined by something called intimacy.

What exactly is intimacy? Well, when you hear the word *intimacy*, you might think of the kind of relationship you'd have with a boyfriend or a girlfriend or a husband or wife, but *intimacy* is actually a general term that refers to a kind of extreme closeness where we share parts of ourselves that we wouldn't share with just anybody. Having an intimate relationship means two people are making themselves vulnerable. These kinds of relationships allow us to learn new things about ourselves, to challenge ourselves to be patient, affectionate and compassionate, and to appreciate other people's viewpoints. These are qualities boys and girls and men and women all need to cultivate to have content and happy lives.

Let's Get Close: Family and Friends

The first intimate relationships we have in our lives are with our caregivers, who, for most people, are parents. Some babies are raised with help from grandparents or older siblings or other family, and some babies are raised with the help of a nanny. No matter who changes our diapers or feeds us or gives us baths, the first people we come in contact with when we're tiny are our first and, in some ways, most important intimate relationships.

Even though we probably can't remember the first months and even years we were alive, the way people talked to us, the way people held us and the way people attended to our needs made a big difference. Babies rely on caregivers to understand what their cries mean, and they need to trust that someone will help them when they need help. Sometimes a baby's cry means "I'm hungry!" and sometimes it means "My diaper is really wet and kind of mushy right now!" but other times it means "I'm feeling lonely—hold me!" So even as babies, we are genetically programmed to want to be understood, and we have an innate sense of trust that someone will both understand us and be able to help us get our needs met, which is actually the core of any good relationship. And just think: it starts when we're too young to even remember it!

As we get older, we have meaningful relationships with the people who continue to feed us, provide us with clothing and a place to live, help us grow and learn new things and have fun with us. For many of us, our parents, siblings and extended family are our main relationships when we're little. When we start going to school, we make friends and form new relationships with people our own age, and we find that we want to pursue relationships with people who have the same interests we do. We want to participate in conversations about things  we have in common, and we start to open up to people about who we really are. These are relationships that are close and meaningful. They are intimate.

Relationships change throughout your life. My brother and I did a lot of things together when we were little, but as he got older and his interests spread out from mine, we had fewer moments of intimate connection and more moments of just being siblings in the same family, which is normal and also fine. I was super close with my mom and dad when I was little, but as I made friends and found things I liked to do, I spent less time with them and more time in my room reading and playing with friends. This is also normal!

It is healthy for relationships to change, and the great thing about strong intimate relationships with family and friends is that there is always a solid core of connection to come back to. There have been times as an adult when I needed my brother almost more than I needed him when we were kids, even though we haven't been as close all of these years. We can draw on our connection as adults in new and important ways now.

The intimacy we feel with family and friends is special and valuable. It is the foundation of all of the relationships we end up having with new people we meet as we grow. Some of the people we meet will become part of a separate kind of intimate relationship: a romantic intimate relationship. But those are not the only relationships that are important to think about as you continue Boying Up.

Brotherhood

One of the closest relationships boys have as they are Boying Up is with their friends: their buddies, their bros, their homeboys, their dudes, their posse. No matter what guys call each other, the friendship of a group of boys and men is intimate and special, even if you don't automatically think of the things a lot of guys like to do together as intimate or special. Groups of boys sometimes play sports and video games when they hang out, but they also can share a fondness for things like sci-fi movies, comic books, music and poetry—really anything at all. In my junior high, I was in orchestra, and a lot of the guys who were in orchestra and jazz band hung out together discussing and playing jazz music. Some guys in my high school were "theater geeks," and they would spend a lot of time rehearsing scenes for plays and choreographing dances for performances. All of these guys' relationships were different, but all shared a notion of a brotherhood that is very important for the Boying Up you are doing.

While girls' relationships are sometimes thought of as a bit more emotionally complicated than friendships between guys, the old-fashioned idea that boys and men don't have complicated relationships or don't need to think about interactions the way women do is exactly that: it's old-fashioned. Boys and men have different ways they handle relationships, but they are just as important and worthy of exploration as girls'.

Evaluating a Friendship

Have you ever had a friend who tells other people things about you that you've asked him to keep private? Do you have a friend who acts one way when it's just the two of you but acts totally different when other people are around? Or someone who's mean to people and assumes you will go along with it? Have you ever had a friend try to pressure you into doing things such as smoke, use drugs, drink or look at inappropriate stuff on the internet? If you answered yes to any of these questions, you may want to reevaluate the friendship. Friends should absolutely help us be the best we can be, and deception, lying and peer pressure are not

> cool. Talk to someone you trust if you think you're in a friendship
> that's not healthy. The way you Boy Up to be the best you that you
> can be is by consistently putting yourself in healthy situations that
> build you and others up.

One of the cool things that happens when guys spend a lot of time together in groups is that they bolster each other in positive ways. The chemicals and hormones of boys and men, especially in their teen years and 20s, makes for a sort of "strength in numbers" that is very easy to see; a great example is guys who play sports together: you get motivated by adrenaline and endorphins and many men report accomplishing things with the support of a group that they could never imagine accomplishing alone. A similar sense of brotherhood happens when men serve in the military together; there is a shared feeling of purpose, motivation and willingness to put their very lives on the line for each other. This kind of brotherhood can lead to tremendous closeness and joy.

However, while it is true that the chemicals and hormones that get released when boys and men work together are powerful and can be transformative and meaningful, it is also true that they can encourage a lot of behaviors that can be harmful or dangerous, when something one boy might be uncomfortable doing on his own seems like it's okay because all of his friends are doing it—or are encouraging him to do it. The saying "boys will be boys" is sometimes used to excuse inexcusable behavior by boys and men (like getting into fights or saying or doing hurtful things to girls), and it's time for us to stop condoning bad behavior as "normal." It's not normal for men to be abusive. It's not normal for men to be disrespectful. It's not normal for men to not listen when someone says "stop," whether it is "stop touching me," "stop talking to me that way," "stop texting me" or even "stop teasing me." The purpose of our communication and ability for closeness as humans means it is all of our responsibilities to speak up when we see people mistreating each other.

Another extension of "boys will be boys" involves the way guys sometimes talk when they are out of earshot of women. It is a normal thing for boys and men to take notice of women and be curious about their bodies, their interests and their potential as partners. However, the way boys and men speak about women absolutely impacts the way girls and women are perceived and treated. Think about it this way: if you have to visit a family member and in the months leading up to the visit you tell yourself how much you don't want to go, and you think about how much you resent going and how much you dislike this person, by the time it's time to visit them, you will be in a pretty negative space. Your mind will effectively be "closed" to the possibility of seeing this person or the situation any other way.

The same could be said to be true of how boys and men are assumed to talk about women. "Locker room talk" that is degrading to women reduces women to sex objects, focuses around misusing their love and their bodies, and brings them down leads to a general mindset that sees women in a negative light. And just as it is not okay to call African American, Jewish or Asian people hurtful names, it is harmful and insensitive to speak harshly about homosexuals or to call boys you don't like "gay" as an insult. In addition, calling a boy names typically used to describe female genitalia (such as pussy or vagina) or calling anyone a bitch is degrading to women and men, and it's vulgar and gross. Basically, if you wouldn't say it in front of your mom or sister or grandma, chances are it's not something smart to say at all.

Even if you don't participate in this kind of talk, being around it and being surrounded by it can have a negative impact on you. Ways to combat this are to reduce the time you spend with boys and men who use disrespectful speech and to spend your energy experiencing positive women and seeing the power and impact

they have on your life, your community and the world. Instead of joining in and teasing someone everyone calls gay, introduce yourself to them and find out about them. Everyone's got a story that deserves to be heard. There should be no hierarchy among boys that sets people who are different below those who blend in more. While it may sound silly—or even impossible—to combat negative locker room talk, you are in charge of how you think and how you treat people. Surround yourself with guys who choose to be in charge the same way.

Fraternity Culture

One of the ways that young men can choose to bolster their male friendships and make new friends in college is by joining a social network of people who live together in apartment buildings and houses, known as fraternities for young men and sororities for young women. These groups require that you pay an annual fee to participate, and they historically do charity work and foster friendships, which can inspire many wonderful things because of the brotherhood that makes boys stronger together. However, the past 20 years or so have revealed many problems with what has become known as "frat boy culture." The way you get into a fraternity (called initiation) has taken on dangerous and harmful elements in many cases, with a lot of drinking and encouraging each other to do things that can be very destructive. While this is not true of every fraternity or sorority, if you think about joining a fraternity, know that being asked to do anything dangerous as part of initiation is not healthy or necessary. In addition, the culture of many fraternities and sororities involves a lot of alcohol consumption, and when alcohol is consumed, judgment can slip, especially that of underage drinkers, whose frontal cortex, the part of the brain that guides judgment, is not fully developed. So if you decide to join a fraternity, be careful about which one you choose, and if anything ever feels weird or like there might be danger or compromising of your ethics, speak up.

Let's Get Even Closer: The Science of Romance

I'm sure you've had a crush on someone or know someone who has, right? I remember having crushes when I was a kid and teenager, and I still have crushes—it's a part of being human, no matter how old you are. With a crush, there's an excitement you feel in your stomach and a nervousness you have when you're around the

person you are crushing on. Crushes are a way that our brains and bodies start getting us used to the idea of liking someone enough to think we might be interested in getting closer to them. Crushes can start because we think someone is cute or funny or just really super cool, and crushes are the earliest stages of romantic intimacy, which is what happens if a crush develops into dating and all of the stuff that comes along with dating.

A lot of what you experience when you are feeling love toward someone has a basis in the brain and the body. The brain releases chemicals to our bodies when we have these kinds of very powerful feelings. If you're experiencing them for the first time, they can also be kind of scary!

When you feel romantically interested in someone, you might feel nervous around them. These are some of the things that might happen when you're nervous:

- Sweating, especially the palms of the hands and underarms
- Dry mouth
- A flushed face and lips that may feel kind of warm and may look pink or red (basically blushing!)
- An increased heart rate, sometimes to the point that it feels like your heart is going to beat right out of your chest
- Having difficulty finding words . . . stuttering, stammering and sometimes sort of babbling

- Feeling disoriented, as if you don't know what is
  going on or who else is around besides the person
  you are focusing on

All of these things are normal responses to being attracted to someone. The nervous system is sending information to the body to indicate that there is excitement going on. When that happens, adrenaline (a hormone) is sent out from glands above your kidneys to increase heart rate and blood flow—that's responsible for the blushing and rapidly beating heart and also the sweating. The "out of it" feeling is caused by a sort of overload that the brain experiences when there is a lot of exciting input happening at once. If we're focusing on someone's beautiful clear blue eyes or their adorable freckles, our brain sometimes has a hard time also managing to multiply fractions or remember which kind of ancient Roman columns have floral decoration on top (Corinthian!). It can feel really disorienting to have our brain so taken over by feelings, but that's just the way it is—and it's how Mother Nature designed it.

When we really like someone or find someone really attractive, our brains produce a group of special hormones that make our bodies feel good. It's those feel-good hormones that make us want to spend more time with that person so that we can experience more of that feeling good more of the time. This is the basis for wanting to be around someone when we like them!

Serotonin is the hormone that is responsible for making us feel super good, and the feeling of "walking on air" when we are with someone we like is due in part to this hormone. If you've ever felt totally crazy about someone, you know what I'm talking about. Oxytocin is the hormone that makes your stomach feel like it's turning upside down when you see someone you like. Oxytocin is also responsible for acting on parts of the body that are involved in the biological process of romantic relationships. So feeling a sensation of "heat" in your chest and in your genital region is often a part of being attracted to someone. It doesn't *always* happen, but it's pretty normal if it does.

Dopamine is a powerful hormone that is released when people have a strong need to be with someone and they get the opportunity to do that. It's known as a "reward" hormone, because it's the body's way of rewarding us with good feelings for doing something we have been working hard to do. This hormone is special because it has an addictive quality; we want to feel a rush of dopamine over and over again once we've gotten a taste of it. This hormone is what makes us seek out our crush over and over again!

THAT'S WHAT HE SAID . . .

"I remember my first crush when I was around 7. I remember she was so pretty—she looked similar to the wives of sports heroes I looked up to. That was attractive to me at the time. Just getting to touch this girl's shoulder when we were in line at school was so

significant to me. There was another boy who also had a crush on her and he would also try to get close to her, and it made me feel so competitive. I wanted to be the one to touch her shoulder!"

Magnetic Feelings: Attraction

So we know we can feel close to people, and we know those feelings can cause changes in our bodies. But how do we know who we will find attractive? How can we prepare for that? Or can we?!

Have you ever thought about what makes someone attractive? What do *you* find attractive?

When I was in middle school, most girls I knew liked guys who were athletic and tall and muscle-y (or as muscle-y as 14-year-old guys can be . . .). Blond hair for guys was "in," and a lot of girls were interested in tan guys who took good care of their hair and clothes, and wore cologne. The first time I ever had serious romantic feelings for someone was in the 8th grade. He was a scrawny, pale-skinned 13-year-old with half-shaved messy black hair, who possibly didn't even look in the mirror every day and didn't ever wear cologne. His name was Mischa, and he liked punk rock and wore a leather jacket. I composed poems for him, picked flowers for him and sat 15 feet away from him in the hallways at recess and lunch for years—even through high school—hoping he'd notice me. He never really did.

Even though Mischa looked and acted so differently from what most other girls I knew thought was attractive, it was very clear to me why I thought the sun rose and set on his green eyes and wacky shaggy hair: he was very smart, he was really funny, and he had a way of doing his own thing and not caring if other people didn't like it, which I thought was spectacular.

I tell this story about my affection for Mischa to illustrate an important point: attraction is highly variable. Sure, there are certain things that are universally considered attractive, but there are also a lot of variations on attractiveness depending on what country you live in, what year it is, what religious tradition and cultural background you're from and what images you see on TV and in the movies. Just like everyone has different favorite colors or favorite foods, we also have different things we find interesting or attractive in other people.

In addition, what's considered attractive in America is not necessarily what's considered attractive in Africa or China or South America or in Polynesia. In many parts of the world, men who are super hairy are considered attractive, while in the United States, more and more men are spending a lot of time and energy waxing, sculpting and shaving. And in some countries, men who are short are seen as just as attractive as tall men, whereas in the United States, tall men are generally ranked as more attractive partners, as are wealthy men. This stuff is all variable—and I know plenty of not-super-tall, not-super-rich men who are wonderful people, whom other people find attractive and who lead happy and fulfilled lives!

Here's the thing: there are no rules about what attractive is. Some people find brains far more important than beauty, and sometimes we will find something attractive that, a year from now, we can't even imagine feeling that way about at all! The notion of what makes someone attractive is not simply how they make our genitals feel; it's about a lot more than that. Sometimes someone with a smart brain and a wicked sense of humor stirs something in our soul that makes us feel like we want to be around that person all of the time, no matter what they look like. And sometimes someone will be so physically attractive that they will make us feel drawn to them, but when we find out that they are mean or cruel or have no manners, they will all of a sudden seem really unattractive. Thank goodness there are no rules about any of this, because even though no one else understood my affection for Mischa, it was a special time in my life to experience those things. I'm glad I didn't let other people's opinions govern my behavior.

Dating

Now that we understand a little bit better what attraction is and what it does to our bodies and brains, let's talk about what happens after we're attracted to someone. In most cultures, the next step after attraction is dating, which means different things to different people and also varies a lot depending on where you live or where your family is from.

Dating generally means spending concentrated time with someone we are attracted to, but for most of human history, romantic love or being attracted to someone was not a requirement for dating. I know that must sound strange, but parents used to set their kids up with a mate for life based on arrangements between the families. Sometimes you were set up to marry someone simply because your families' wheat fields were next to one another or because one father was another father's best friend. In many of these cases, marriages were basically business agreements between two fathers. Women were essentially treated as property, and they usually didn't get a vote as to whom they would marry. There are many communities in the world where arranged marriage is still the way couples get together. In addition, for much of human history, men were allowed to have more than one wife, and there are places where this still happens, such as parts of the Middle East, Asia, Africa and Australia.

Most of us meet prospective romantic partners at school, through community activities, through extracurriculars and through hanging out with friends. I spent a lot of time in my middle school and high school years in malls, arcades and friends' living rooms chatting with all of the boys I had crushes on. But dating has changed a lot since I was in school. Because of smartphones and social media, dating now involves texting and following, liking and commenting on the different things people post online. You can learn a lot about someone from online profiles in ways I never could when I was dating. There are some great things about that, but there are some challenges, too.

Even though your parents must seem like dinosaurs to you, they were your age around 30 years ago, and considering that *Homo sapiens* have been around for about 200,000 years, 30 years isn't that long ago! But the thing that makes talking about dating so hard is how much it changes all of the time—there have been so many changes just in the years since your parents and I were your age. Here's a rundown of what dating used to be like and what it's like now, with a special emphasis on making the most of the good changes while learning to navigate the potentially problematic ones.

NICE TO MEET YOU

THEN: It used to be that you dated people from your social circles: people you knew from school or your family's religious events or from sports teams or clubs you belonged to. Chances are, if you met someone, your parents already knew them, and if your parents didn't, someone in your family or circle of friends did.

NOW: There are so many ways to meet people! Besides meeting people at school and at extracurricular activities, you can meet online. Social-media platforms and comments sections are virtual hangout spaces, an entire world of online communities where people now connect, and are a place to meet.

PRECAUTIONARY POINTERS: Meeting people online can be a neat way to expand the circle of people you know and can date, but keep in mind that the way people present themselves online is not always the way they actually are, and in some cases, people blatantly lie about who they are, how old they are and what they're all about. Sometimes people make things up about themselves so they can get you interested in them. Because they only show us what they want us to see, the way people share about themselves online can make us feel like we know them, but in reality, we don't. That's just the nature of the online beast!

HOW TO BE SMART ABOUT IT: If you meet someone online, the best way to really get to know if that someone is potentially a good date, or even just a possible new friend, is to meet them in person in a public place—but only with your parents' knowledge and consent. You should never go out with someone you met online without an adult knowing where you are. Anyone who asks you to keep a secret about meeting up should for sure be avoided. That's what we call in my house a "prickly" person; prickly people ask you to keep secrets from those close to you, and they are not safe people to hang out with.

COURTSHIP: WHAT'S THAT?!

THEN: *Courtship* is the old-fashioned word for the way two people who are dating get to know each other. The super old-school version of this sounds like a TV show from the 1950s: a young man comes to a girl's house with flowers and sits and chats with her dad while she finishes getting ready. The idea is that the guy is supposed to impress the girl and her family, and their dating is an elaborate way for him to show he has good intentions and wants to spend more time with her, eventually landing him the chance to ask her father for permission to marry her.

While the idea that a guy needs a girl's dad's approval to date her and marry her sounds so out of date and kind of absurd, what is kind of sweet about the notion of courtship is this: it takes time to get to know someone. It takes time to see what it's like to be together if you're interested in a more serious relationship. It takes time to build up trust in order to let someone see more of you and to eventually engage in an intimate or romantic relationship that at some point may involve hand holding, kissing and—yes, eventually many people choose to be sexually intimate! And this kind of courtship shows that it is important for your family to know the person you're dating and for them to spend time together at some point.

NOW: This is an area of dating that is completely different in almost every way compared to how it used to be! While there are still places in the world where a guy comes to the door to pick a girl up for a date and chats with her dad before he can take her out, a lot of courtship does not look anything like that anymore. Courtship now sometimes means rarely actually talking; texting and sending each other pictures may be a large part of the courtship process. Many people think that dating doesn't need to be a stepping-stone to a serious relationship but should just be for fun.

PRECAUTIONARY POINTERS: What's potentially problematic about the loss of a notion of courtship is that we basically think we can and should trust people before we even know much about them. People may say things we want to hear, but we have no idea if they plan to follow through with promises, since they haven't necessarily had to put time and effort in to show that they are reliable or faithful or honest. It can be confusing and hard to know who to trust sometimes.

Also, an aspect of the courtship process that never existed before now is sending someone you like "sexy" pictures of yourself or asking others to send "sexy" pictures for you to see. I totally get why this is commonplace, especially since we see so many celebrities posting pictures of themselves on their social media accounts in lingerie, skimpy bathing suits and sometimes even naked! It's no wonder it's become something expected or assumed to be part of getting to know someone and flirting.

The problem with sending sexy pictures or sexting with someone (talking about sexy stuff in texts) is that the pictures live forever on someone's phone, and pictures sent to one particular person might end up being shared with a bunch of people—we've all shared or known someone who shared a picture they probably were not supposed to share with us. You can do your part as a brave, bold and brilliant person by not engaging in this kind of photo sharing as much as possible. Avoid the pressure to turn sexy pictures of girls and women into an activity. Putting that kind of energy into ogling women sets you—and them—up to see relationships as a display of sexuality. I know it seems like I am overreacting, but I hope you can start to consider that this is not just paranoia; it's based on years and years of experience and reading a ton of research on the impact of these kinds of interactions.

HOW TO BE SMART ABOUT IT: The more time you spend with someone in person—and not just texting—the better you can see if you like actually being with them. Having a friendship or relationship that involves sharing pictures and flirting is fun, but you want to make sure that there is a good amount of time spent in person, seeing how you feel when the two of you are together. In addition, some of that old-fashioned courtship stuff is nice; it can show that you think the other person is worthy of your time and respect. That's a very important aspect of dating for both people involved. The kinds of relationships you want to have will be with people you like spending time with and people you can trust with your feelings; it's best to see who wants to put that effort in early on!

LET'S TALK ABOUT S-E-X

In Chapter One, we talked about the mechanics of the body and how sperm is produced in the testes all of the time. We also talked about how girls' and women's bodies produce an egg every month or so that travels from their ovaries through the fallopian tubes and waits in the uterus to potentially develop into a baby.

How the act of sex actually happens is that the penis fills up with blood because of a state of excitement called "arousal," which we discussed earlier in this chapter; this is an erection. When a female is aroused, her nipples sometimes stand up a little bit, and blood flows into her vagina, particularly into the clitoris, which is the most sensitive part of a woman's genital region. Sex is when an erect penis moves back and forth inside of the vagina. After a while, the penis releases sperm in an act called ejaculation. Ejaculation produces millions of sperm (they are very tiny, so they take up about one teaspoon), and they actually exist in a fluid called semen, which allows the sperm to survive. Ejaculation releases semen (and therefore sperm) into the highest part of the vagina near where the vagina meets the uterus at a location called the cervix. The goal of sperm is to find an egg to fertilize. Each sperm has a head that contains all of its genetic information, and it has a tail that moves back and forth really fast and propels it through the woman's vagina in search of an egg.

If an egg is fertilized, it can implant in the uterus and begin forming what will in 9 or 10 months become a human baby. The process is amazing, and it is unbelievable that a sperm meeting an egg can lead to a human growing inside of a woman's body!

Let's talk about how people have behaved surrounding the idea of sex and how you can prepare for one day deciding how you want to handle sex and all that it entails.

THEN: Historically, people of certain religious and cultural backgrounds—as well as a lot of others not from a particular religious or cultural background—have waited to have sex until they are married. For your grandparents' and great-grandparents' generations, that was not unusual at all. The idea that your body is a sacred place may sound weird now, but for a lot of history, being sexually intimate with someone was considered in many communities to be something you didn't do until marriage. Of course there have always been people who have been sexually active before marriage, but one of the main reasons the act of sex was saved for marriage is the simple fact that women are likely to get pregnant if they have sex! It's just a biological fact. Until very recently, sex was seen by many as just a way to make babies, which for most cultures was encouraged to be done in the context of marriage so that a woman could be provided for while she cared for her babies. Many religions and cultures made a big deal over seeing sex as "forbidden," often because of the possibility of getting pregnant outside of marriage. In certain religious traditions, such as Catholicism and some Eastern religions, leaders of the faith take vows of celibacy (not having sex) for part of their lives and sometimes for their entire lives, because sex is seen as a potential distraction.

NOW: There are still many people who believe that sex is something you save for marriage, but for many young people in this country, there has been a real shift in the past 60 years in how we see ourselves and how we behave sexually. There are many reasons for this shift, and one of them is that in 1960, a birth control pill (referred to as "the Pill") was introduced that could stop women from releasing an egg, thus making it possible for them to control when they got pregnant—or didn't. The Pill changed the world in ways we are still learning to understand. Since the 1960s and what is sometimes called the "sexual revolution," the notion of "waiting for marriage" has shifted a lot.

What this looks like is that a lot of young people—many of you reading this book, actually—may be comfortable with things that girls and boys and men and women even 15 years ago would not have been comfortable with. Kissing used to be something many of your parents wondered if they "should" do on a first date, and now I'm sure you know that kissing can happen before you even decide that you are dating! Hooking up is something that sometimes happens even between people with no interest in dating. Having sex is seen by some as not a big deal, and some people think it's something you should do just because it feels good.

PRECAUTIONARY POINTERS: It would be super awkward for me to just come right out and say, "Don't hook up with people you barely know!" "Wait until you know someone before you let them kiss you!" "Don't have sex before you're in a committed relationship!" I know for a lot of people that's not going to make sense, and I get that. Here's the truth: every time you come in physical contact with someone by kissing them, touching them or being sexually intimate with them, you are opening yourself up to the history of who they have been intimate with. Even when we just kiss someone and share body fluids—which is what happens when we kiss!—our bodies have ways they react.

This is something to keep in mind anytime you are sexually intimate with someone, even just by kissing them. I'm not saying that if you kiss someone, you're going to get sick, but the principle is important to know: being intimate in a sexual way is sharing parts of you that can be affected physically in sometimes very serious ways, because coming in contact with someone's penis or vagina or having body fluids exchanged through kissing, oral sex and sexual intercourse is a very significant experience for the body. A great example is that if someone kisses a person who has a cold sore and then they kiss you, you may end up with the cold sore. Anytime anyone's lips and kisses are near any of your mucus membranes (any opening of your body), you can take their germs and the germs they get from other people into your body, and they become a part of you.

A lot of us grow up with notions of sexual intimacy being an emotional experience. But if you look at how a lot of music videos and TV and movies talk about and show sexual situations, it's sometimes treated like it's no big deal. Women are sometimes depicted as acting aggressively in sexual situations, and it's becoming more commonplace for the media to show women as emotionally separated from sexual intimacy. What's absolutely true is that being sexually intimate has a lot of impact on humans, especially on females. Remember all of the hormones we talked about in the earlier chapters? Those are supercharged when we have sex. Even though being sexual is enjoyable, it does change a relationship when we're sexual with someone. Young people especially are not necessarily prepared to deal with some of the feelings that can come up when we have sexual relations with someone. Sometimes we may feel guilty, and sometimes we may feel it wasn't what we expected, and sometimes it can even feel like the other person didn't treat us the way we wanted to be treated.

It's important to acknowledge that having sex is a special thing, and it is a very big deal, and that's not just true for women. Sex is very significant for men and women, and most people you talk to who have a lot of experience in life will tell you that sex is best when it's emotionally connected, not just when you do it as a purely physical act because it feels like the thing to do at the moment or because you think everyone else is doing it.

At the same time, although sex is very important, you shouldn't be afraid of it. Although many religious traditions have very strong opinions about sex for good reasons, and although many parents take the idea of their children's sexual activity very seriously—as they should—sex is not evil. It can be a beautiful way to connect with someone, and I can tell you from personal experience that the most meaningful, awesome sex comes from being in a solid, healthy relationship that involves a lot of trust, a lot of communication about everyone's needs and a lot of tenderness and fun.

HOW TO BE SMART ABOUT IT: I'm going to come right out and tell you that your body is awesome. Your body is made to feel good, and it's made to be a part of starting a family if you want to do that someday. You deserve to feel good. You get to decide who touches you where and when, and no one should ever make you feel bad for not wanting to be sexual (or for wanting to be sexual either). The same is true for any partner you might have. Just as you don't want anyone to make you do something you don't want to do, you should never—*never*—pressure anyone into doing things they aren't ready to do.

Consent

Many images we see in the media and songs we hear talk about the subtle and not-so-subtle ways men can get women to do what they want sexually. In addition, a lot of messages we get tell us that it's a woman's job to please men; it's not. There is a notion in many circles of society, including the world of pornography, that hints—or directly states—that women want sex even when they say they don't. This is not healthy and it's not something to imitate. *"No" means "no."* Period. It can be very difficult, when your hormones are in full force and when you have an erection, to control your desires, but it is your responsibility to listen if someone says no. If someone pushes you away, remove yourself from the situation. It's not a game. And if someone thinks teasing you by pushing you away is an invitation for intimacy, it's okay to say, "Be clear: is this a yes or a no?" One of the reasons many adults encourage young people to wait to be intimate is that when you are young and learning how to control your body and your brain, your judgment is not as sharp as it will be when you mature. Being confronted with a situation where someone says no after they said yes can be very difficult for many young men. Alcohol and drugs can confuse decision-making, especially for underage drinkers, so it is wise to avoid drinking if you want to cultivate a responsible and safe environment as you start to get to know someone.

Every girl and every woman and every partner you may ever have has the right to control their body. And you have the right to control yours, too. No matter what, there is no situation in which anyone has the right to think they can touch or kiss or have sex with someone who doesn't want to or who seems unsure. The notion of consent has nothing to do with the clothes someone wears, the way they flirt with you or even agreeing to be treated to dinner. Sex must be agreed on by both people involved, and if your partner changes their mind regarding how far they want to go at any point during a date, that has to be respected. Forcing someone to engage in any sexual act when they say no or cannot give consent is against the law, and you could spend the rest of your life in jail and ruin someone's life by forcing them to have sex when they don't want to.

If you do decide to be sexually active, know that condoms should be used anytime fluid can enter someone's body from your genitals. Condoms prevent both of you from getting diseases that come from other people's body fluids and can stay with you and affect your life forever. Boys and men can get diseases from girls and women; it doesn't just work the other way around. It's important to understand the ways to prevent sexually transmitted diseases even if you are the guy in the relationship. You can talk to your family doctor, parents or another trusted adult about it. There are some diseases you can get from having sexual relations that never go away. They can affect your ability to have babies later in life. It's scary. And being careful about who you have sex with is very important. Like I said before, people you meet online and know very little about are not safe people just because they say they are. Making smart choices now can have an effect on the rest of your life.

Pregnancy

No one wants to think that they might get someone pregnant if they decide to have sex in high school or middle school, but here's the bottom line. I'm going to be very clear about this: *having sex is what makes a girl get pregnant.* Condoms are very effective against pregnancy if they are used correctly. There are other ways to prevent pregnancy, and there are advantages and disadvantages to all of them. There are people who think if you just have sex for a little time, then you won't get pregnant—they're wrong; that's not safe. If you don't want to get someone pregnant, the best choice is to not put your penis into her vagina. Semen comes out of the penis and carries cells that, when they meet with an egg cell, make a baby. Period.

Contraception

Because of the way male and female bodies work, contraception typically consists of finding ways to stop an egg from meeting sperm, and most methods require action by the female partner, although new methods are being researched which would require men to share more of the responsibility of birth control. As I stated above, the only way to make sure you don't get someone pregnant is pretty clear, but here are the most common types of contraception—and don't skip this section because you are a guy; contraception and preventing diseases that come from being sexually active are everyone's responsibility, not just the woman's. Keep in mind that contraception has to be used correctly in order for it to work as well as it can, and no contraception is 100 percent guaranteed to not let a girl get pregnant. Also know that some sperm can also be released before ejaculation, so the "withdrawal/pull-out" method is not a reliable form of contraception.

Here are a few types that people often use:

Condoms. A condom fits over the penis to catch sperm so they don't get into the vagina. When used correctly, condoms are a very reliable form of birth control.
Most condoms are made of latex, and
you usually need to use a lubricant
with a condom so that the latex doesn't
feel uncomfortable for your partner.
Condoms protect from sexually
transmitted diseases by creating a barrier
between two bodies; this is something
that only condoms provide.

The Pill. A birth control pill is prescribed for women by a doctor, and it needs to be taken every day at about the same time in order for it to work. The Pill is made up of hormones that stop the ovaries from sending eggs into the fallopian tubes. The hormones in the Pill are powerful, and some women feel a bit more moody and emotional than usual when they are on the Pill.

Hormonal patch and hormonal rings. Patches are like Band-Aids that contain the same kinds of hormones that are in the Pill. A patch has to be placed by the woman on her body and removed at set times or it doesn't work. The hormonal ring is inserted into the vagina and stays there securely. The way the hormones are delivered for both of these methods tends to lead to fewer side effects than the Pill.

Other birth control: IUD, shots, sterilization. These are more invasive and complicated methods of birth control, which are typically not recommended for teenagers. Some women have an intrauterine device (IUD) implanted in their uterus. Another method of birth control for women is hormonal injections, which stop the release of eggs. Finally, when both partners are sure that they don't ever want to have babies, there are surgical procedures for both men and women that make them not able to do so.

Self-Discovery

We've talked a lot about what happens when you touch someone else, but there's another kind of touching too. When you touch yourself, it's called masturbation. While some cultures and religions have strong opinions about masturbation not being healthy or good, it is widely accepted that there is nothing wrong with touching yourself; your body was designed with parts that feel good when they are touched, and that's very important! At different times in your life, you may have more or less interest in masturbating, but pretty much everyone does it, and it's totally okay to learn about your body in this way. Sometimes, you may have what is called a nocturnal emission, or a "wet dream," and wake up to realize you have ejaculated. This is also normal, and it's nothing to worry about. If you have concerns or questions about masturbation or ejaculation, a doctor or school nurse can help. A lot of times, guys share information about their bodies, and that might also help you get your questions answered . . . but keep in mind that some boys like to exaggerate and make things up . . . so if something sounds hard to believe, you might want to run it by an adult you trust!

Late Bloomers

Did anyone read this chapter and think, *What is she talking about?!* Or, *Eeeww! I don't want to talk about this stuff!* Or maybe, *I don't want to think about sex, and I don't even want to think about going on a date!* If so, that's totally fine! Everyone matures at a different pace, and the way you are is exactly the way you are supposed to be.

I don't even know if I could have gotten through this chapter when I was your age, because I was a late bloomer. Like, a super late bloomer.

I developed late. I was really short, and I didn't start my menstrual cycle until late in high school—girls usually start around age 12. I was not interested in dating, and I had my first kiss when I was acting in a TV show when I was 14. I didn't have my first real boyfriend until I was 17, and I never "casually" dated. I never hooked up with guys at camp or at school; I have had only long-term relationships, and I believe very strongly in having one committed partner at a time.

You might be thinking I have no clue what dating is like or that I have no right to comment on it since I was a clueless teenager. But here's the thing: I didn't engage in that stuff because I wasn't ready, and that's okay. I was really freaked out when I learned about the diseases you can get from fooling around.

The truth is, being a late bloomer turned out to be a good thing for me. The fact that I was left out of a lot of jokes and conversations because I couldn't relate didn't end up affecting me much in the long run. I have never met someone who hooked up with a lot of people who felt it made them better equipped to have a healthy relationship or marriage later in life—it was just a different path to getting there. One path isn't necessarily better than

How Boys Love

the other or a better predictor of your success in relationships or in the bedroom. Keep that in mind when people say things like, "If you want to learn how to be a good kisser, you need a lot of practice," because that's simply not true. And that's also the case for a lot of things people will say, such as, "The only way to be a good lover is to practice a lot." It's also not true. Being a good lover and partner is about being in touch with your feelings and your needs, and wanting to be there for someone you care about and have strong feelings for. You get to take your time with how fast or slow that happens.

I know that being a late bloomer saved me from a lot of the drama and heartache that can come from having lots of relationships, but people who experienced a lot of relationships can learn from them, and that's fine, too. For me, as a very sensitive and vulnerable person, the brief experiences I've had with the ups and downs of trying to get people to like me and date me and then feeling let down and rejected if they didn't was enough to turn me off from pursuing it more. I spent a lot of time in middle school and high school studying, playing and listening to music and writing letters to friends. I liked reading and writing poetry, and while I sometimes felt lonely, looking back, I spent time learning the things I like and things I don't like, and I wouldn't change my being a late bloomer for anything. For all of the late bloomers out there who might feel they are missing out on something: it may seem like you are, but trust me, everyone progresses in their own way in their own time, and it's important

127

to listen to your gut. We all get there eventually, and it is very important for you to honor your intuition and to always go at your own pace.

On *The Big Bang Theory*, I play a late bloomer who didn't have sex until she was well into her adult life. My character, Amy, had been dating Sheldon for years before he was ready to have a first kiss with her, and she had never kissed anyone before! Amy decided that being patient and waiting until Sheldon was ready was important, and it was an indication of her love for him. Sheldon, in the 9th season of our show, decided to make his birthday gift for Amy the gift of sexual intimacy. Amy was really shocked, and she and Sheldon were both nervous when they decided to make their relationship sexual. Sheldon said a sweet thing. He said, "We can find out together." And they did.

We all figure it out one way or the other. The thing I've treasured most about my late-bloomer journey is being able to take a lot of time to make decisions and to weigh whether my choices felt right or not. I used to feel ashamed that I was such a late bloomer, but now I embrace it.

THAT'S WHAT HE SAID . . .

"My sister is 15 months younger than me, and we had a joint party for her Bat Mitzvah and my Bar Mitzvah (she was 12; I was 13). But she was taller than me because at that age girls go into puberty before boys,

and I recall needing a box to stand on to see over the lectern. I remember having a complex about that; I'm taller than her now, so as I grew and saw that I wasn't going to be that short for the duration of my life, I got some more confidence."

Wrapping Up

Understanding your body and how it relates to intimacy is an important part of Boying Up because learning how your emotions and feelings impact other people is what will make you a wonderful friend, son, sibling, boyfriend and husband, if that's what you choose to be.

Know that your feelings and your body can help you communicate some of the most profound and life-changing things we get to experience as humans. A lot of what this chapter covered revolves around the question "What kind of boy and man do you want to be?" People like to be around someone who behaves politely, acts with respect toward people and models qualities of responsibility, consistency and strength of character. While you may see "bad boys" getting attention in the tween and teen years—and even into your 20s and beyond—know that behaving with kindness and generosity is always attractive. Boys who respect girls and women become men who do the same.

Surround yourself with healthy examples of men and women.

Avoid thinking that your popularity is the most important thing you have going for you. In the long run, a Boying Up journey that is worth taking is one of dignity, wisdom and fostering the kinds of relationships with those around you that inspire confidence, meaning and love.

FIVE

• HOW BOYS COPE •

The transition from boy to young man, which I've called Boying Up, is an exciting one. Being alive at this time in history is so awesome, and there is a lot to celebrate.

But is life all about awesomeness and celebration? Is everything always wonderful and smooth sailing?

When I watch TV or go to the movies, or when I look on social media, I see a lot of spectacular things and super-happy people. I see people with smiling families, adorable pets, beautiful houses, supportive friends, loving relationships and what often look like perfect lives. The things people post show a world of joy and success. But that's not what life is always like. Bad things happen. We get sad. Situations come up that we don't always know how to handle. And sometimes it can feel like, if our life isn't the way other people's lives look, there's something wrong with us.

Psychologists and sociologists are experts on why and how people do the things they do, and they have defined the following things as the most challenging and prone to make us feel stressed out:

- Moving to a new house or apartment
- Death of someone close to you
- Divorce in your family
- Problems with money in your family

What are some other things that can be stressful?

- Breaking up with someone or having a fight with a close friend
- Having romantic feelings for someone who doesn't feel them back
- Being teased or bullied for being different
- Pressure from parents to do well in school
- Difficult relationships with siblings or other family members
- Having a family member in the military
- Hearing in the news about some of the stuff that's going on in the world

Even though these things are not as stressful as death or divorce or moving or money problems, they are still stressful, and they can affect us in big ways.

What Is Stress?

So what exactly is stress? What does it do, and how does it change us?

The word is sometimes used to describe the pressure of, say, a bowling ball resting on a flimsy table; the table is under the stress of a super-heavy weight—that's physical stress. Emotional stress is not so different. It's the pressure we feel when we've been put  in a really difficult, challenging situation. Stress affects the body and the brain, and stress can also affect the way we deal with people around us and the things we have to do, even if they have nothing to do with the actual thing that's stressing us out. So being stressed about one thing can turn into being stressed about a lot of things; in that way, stress kind of grows.

Stressful situations can be physical, such as being approached by an angry dog who looks like he's ready to attack you. Or stressful things can affect feelings and behavior, such as the loss of someone we love. When we are challenged physically, our brains get the message that something needs attention and that we have to do something about it, usually right away. There is a part of the brain called the amygdala that is responsible for us feeling fear and knowing what to do when things are scary. So if we are approached by an angry dog, this triggers the amygdala, and it says, "Yikes! Holy moly: DOG!" The next thing that happens is our amygdala starts communicating with the rest of the brain to initiate things that will help us protect ourselves from this threat.

If you've ever heard of the expression "fight or flight," you have an idea of what your brain is responsible for when it feels it's under attack. The body sends extra blood to our muscles so that we can either use our muscles to defend ourselves (if we choose to fight) or to run away (if we choose to engage in getting the heck out of there, also known as flight). Our brains send information to our hearts to pump extra blood, and this raises our heart rate and blood pressure. Our brains also send hormones, such as adrenaline, norepinephrine and cortisol for energy and to give us the confidence to protect ourselves, into our blood. These hormones and the increase in blood flow to the heart explain the fluttery feeling you might have experienced if you've ever been scared or threatened. (It also happens when you see someone you have a crush on, but for slightly different reasons!)

So our bodies perceive stressful things as threats that need to be fixed one of two ways: by fighting or by running away.

Here's a diagram of some parts of our brain and what they do.

But what about emotional stress? How does that get handled by our brains and bodies?

To the brain, emotional stress is actually not that different from a physical threat. When we encounter an emotionally threatening or stressful situation, the brain gets a message: stressful situation happening! And even though emotional or psychological stress may

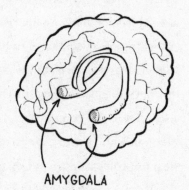

AMYGDALA

be different from a one-time event such as an angry dog approaching you, the brain still starts sending out hormonal messengers into the body to start protecting us from what the brain interprets as an emotional attack.

The difference when we experience an emotionally or psychologically stressful situation is caused by the fact that the brain keeps trying to support us for however long a situation is happening. For example, if you have a family member in the military, you are going to have some strong feelings about it. You might feel sad, and you might miss that person. You might be scared for their safety, and you may take an extra interest in the news so you can see if the place they are stationed is ever mentioned. These are all real concerns, and they are stressful for sure. Your brain will be on alert for a long time—until your loved one comes back from the military. It's not a one-time thing; it's a prolonged stress.

The amazing thing about the brain is that it can provide support in ways that will help you be able to function at school and at home so that kind of prolonged stress won't take over your whole life. The brain can process more than one thing at a time! The way it does this is by allowing us to be distracted, even for short periods of time, by tasks at school, parties we're invited to and daily things that need to get done such as chores and being a productive part of activities. In this way, we can have something we are stressed about going on while we also can enjoy things and continue our lives even with this constant stressful thing going on in the back of our minds, as it were.

Here's the catch, though: everyone's brain works slightly differently, and everyone reacts differently to stress. So for some people, the death of a family pet might make them feel devastated for a week but then they can get back to "normal" life and mostly feel unaffected by it. They might still miss their pet and get sad from time to time, but for the most part, they will feel fine about it after a short time. This is totally normal. For other people, the death of a pet might stay with them for a long time. They may feel sad for months. This is also totally normal.

The differences in how people react to stress depend on a lot of things. Genetics and what kinds of personality features you inherited from your parents come into play. So do the environment and how your family taught you to understand feelings and what to do with them. Your reactions also depend on things you have control over, such as emotional skills you can use to help you get through hard times. In addition, stress is cumulative, which means when stresses happen, they add up, especially if you didn't work through previous stresses completely. So stressors can pile on top of each other and produce even bigger reactions than we might have had if we were only dealing with one stressful thing at a time.

Do Boys and Girls Feel Emotions the Same?

It's important to know that even though male and female brains are not identical, the processing of stress and emotions is not terribly different in boys versus girls. So even though a lot of people might assume that girls get more upset about things than boys, much of the way we think about boys and girls comes from our culture, not from our genetics or our brain anatomy. Stressful situations have the ability to impact boys just as much as girls. If you lose someone you love, your brain processes that as a loss whether you are a boy or a girl. If someone calls you hurtful names or consistently targets you and bullies you, it's very painful. If you feel people don't understand you and you have a constant sense of feeling different, that's a big deal. And if you like someone who doesn't like you back, it hurts your heart, no matter what. Crying would be a normal response to any of these things—no matter if you are a boy or a girl. It is a cultural expectation that "boys don't cry." But they can, they do, and they should. Crying is an important mechanism for expressing sadness and grief, and there are even studies showing that the stress hormone cortisol is released when you cry, which is part of what can make you feel better. So why do girls tend to cry and boys don't? It really boils down to the kind of encouragement or discouragement boys are given in a particular culture and family to express feelings. It is completely normal for boys and girls alike to experience every single emotion there is: sadness, joy, rage, fear, disgust, anxiety—you name it, and boys and girls alike feel it! So if you ever worry that you are "too upset" about something stressful, don't stress about being stressed; those are normal feelings, and it's healthy to feel them. Holding things in can cause you mental and physical pain later on. They say feeling and strong emotions are like urine: you can try to keep it in, but sooner or later it's going to come out! So don't be afraid to let those feelings out! And talk to a parent, friend, teacher or an adult you trust.

THAT'S WHAT HE SAID . . .

"Anxiety has been a constant for me in my life. For years, I minimized my emotional experiences by intellectualizing them. I'd have an emotion such as, say, anger and would decide that whatever caused it was not worth getting into an argument over. So, I would 'decide' not to be angry. I used this approach for years— and through therapy, I realized that avoiding emotional experiences was creating a deep well of anxiety in me. I now work hard at experiencing emotions directly, in the moment, and sitting with them even if they make me uncomfortable. I've learned to do a variety of breathing exercises that help me sit with them, and I write in a journal. Most importantly, I have learned that expressing emotions by simply saying something like 'I am angry because . . .' helps me process whatever emotions I have."

• • •

What Does Emotional Stress Look Like?

If we are in a stressful situation that is not about fight or flight but is instead about something emotional, here are some of the things that we may experience, especially if the stress continues for a while or if we are having a hard time understanding how to handle the stress.

1. **Changes to our bodies:**
   - We may lose or gain weight. Some people eat more than they usually do when they are stressed; some people find it hard to eat.
   - We may feel achy or tired a lot.
   - We may find it hard to concentrate or think straight.

2. **Sad feelings:**
   - We may feel hopeless and lose interest in things we previously had interest in, such as hobbies or friends or activities at school.
   - Life may seem "blah," and we may feel like just hanging around rather than going out and doing things. Even getting out of bed or getting dressed can feel like a chore. It may even feel as if we are trudging through mud just to get up and get going.

3. **Angry feelings:**
   - We may feel irritable, short-tempered and angry, sometimes for no apparent reason or out of the blue.

- We may feel like hurting ourselves or other people, or throwing or even breaking things. These symptoms and feelings are the body and brain's reactions to stress. Over time, these feelings can get stronger and stronger, and unless we find ways to deal with them, we can do damage to our bodies, our brains and our relationships.

When Sadness Becomes Depression

Sudden weight loss or weight gain accompanied by prolonged feelings of tiredness, hopelessness and losing interest in things we previously loved doing can also occur in a condition called depression. Depression is different from sadness, and if you are feeling sad and hopeless for longer than 2 weeks, talk to a doctor, parent or trusted teacher about it and tell them you think you may be depressed. In addition, if you find you are feeling intensely sad with nothing stressful going on, talk to someone. There is help for you, and it's very important to talk to someone early on in depression so you can get the help you need before it escalates into a bigger problem that may be harder for you to handle. You can call the National Suicide Prevention Lifeline at 800-273-8255. The Trevor Project also provides mental-health resources specifically for LGBTQ youth, and you can find them at www.thetrevorproject.org or call them at 866-488-7386.

THAT'S WHAT HE SAID . . .

"My most effective treatment for depression is a good night's sleep. While awake, I can spin and spin into increasingly dark places emotionally, but when I fall asleep, it's as if my brain resets. The moment I wake up, I feel clean of all darkness, and for this reason, the moment I wake up is the best time to combat depression with positivity such as making a mental list of things I am grateful for."

Coping

One of the most important things to understand about emotional stress is that there are ways to make it better, even if it seems like nothing will make it better. It's called *coping*. Sadly, a lot of us don't know how to cope in healthy ways. Instead, we may turn to unhealthy ways to cope to try to make ourselves feel better. Here are some common coping mechanisms.

ANGER

Stress can make people feel angry, even if there's nothing that anger can do to make the stress go away. Anger can be a useful emotion when it signals to us that something is wrong or upsetting, and it can motivate us to do things to change the situation. The thing about emotional stress is that it doesn't always go away if we get angry at it. And sometimes people take their anger out on others by yelling at them, hitting them or being mean to them with words and actions. This does not lessen the source of the stress, and in fact it can lead to more stress, even if it makes the angry person feel better in the moment. Being abusive or taking out your anger on others actually triggers more stress in your body over time, so if you see yourself doing this when you're stressed out, take a deep breath and try to come up with some other ways to cope with what's upsetting you. Talking to someone you trust can help a lot, and most everyone has had angry feelings, so know that you're not alone.

Do Women Get as Mad?

What about women? Can they be aggressive like men sometimes get? The short answer is yes. It is normal for both boys and girls and women and men to experience things that enrage them and make them want to be physical to communicate emotions. As boys reach puberty, they typically get a strong flow of the hormones responsible for regulating and monitoring angry and aggressive responses to stress or emotion. Girls don't typically have as much of these hormones as boys do. There are exceptions on both sides, but for the most part, things that make boys and men mad generally make girls and women mad as well. Note to yourself: if a girl or woman looks really mad, don't assume she can't hold her own physically just because she's a girl . . . the hormones that monitor strong and especially angry emotions are very powerful!

When Anger Becomes Violence

It is never okay for someone to hit you or hurt you because they are angry, even if they tell you it's your fault and even if they are your parent or sibling or friend. If you feel scared in your home or in any relationship, you deserve to speak up and be protected. If you're in any sort of abusive situation, or know someone who is, don't hesitate to ask for help. Talk to a trusted adult, or use some of these resources:

- If you're facing abuse at home, you can get help from the National Domestic Violence Hotline at TheHotline.org.

- And if you're in a relationship that is abusive in any way, Loveisrespect offers empowering resources at loveisrespect.org.

If you find that you're the one lashing out physically when you get mad and you notice that people are scared of your anger, talk to a trusted adult or counselor who can help you learn about anger management.

CHANNELING ANGER INTO PRODUCTIVE MOVEMENT

One way to deal with stress in a healthy way is by doing something physical and productive, as opposed to bottling up angry feelings or using violence or aggression. The energy you expend through practicing, training and competing makes for a great release of stress and tension. Athletes sometimes talk about being "in the zone" when they are training, and you sometimes feel a "high" when your body really starts moving. For those of us with a tendency to be stressed out or angry or tense, being physical in sports is a healthy and safe way to burn off excess energy and emotions. Sometimes when I'm really stressed out, I will take a brisk walk or a jog, and I can literally feel the negative feelings leaving my body with every step I take. Being an athlete is not without its stresses, but physical activity is a great way to burn off energy, no matter how you do it.

Using healthy ways to get the brain out of its initial stressful

upset encourages it to send out calming signals to the body. Happy chemicals get woken up that may have been sleeping because of the stress. Once the brain starts to stimulate those chemicals, like serotonin and dopamine, it starts to chip away at all of the sad stuff floating around the brain and body. And the neat thing about these happy hormones is that the brain is kind of addicted to them: once it has a taste of feeling a little bit better, it can start building you up to help you feel better.

DISTRACTION

Sometimes people drink or use drugs or even zone out in front of the TV to avoid dealing with the emotions stressful situations can bring up. Overeating and obsessing about what you eat are also distractions some people use to avoid the feelings that come up in stressful times. These distractions work for the moment, but they don't actually do anything to help us move past those hard feelings. Over time, alcohol and drugs can become a crutch and a danger to your health, and they contribute to making a lot of choices that ultimately can impact your life in damaging ways. Zoning out in front of the TV is sometimes okay as a break from stressing out, but distracting ourselves is not a long-term solution to understanding our feelings and doing productive things with them.

When Someone's Drinking or Drug Use Becomes a Problem

Drugs and alcohol cause significant changes to the brain, even the first time you use them. These substances activate chemicals in your brain that make you feel certain things by hijacking your brain's normal operations. When on drugs or when drinking, some people think they are super strong or super confident, or they develop a craving for feeling "zoned out." Over time, the brain gets addicted to drugs and alcohol, which means that you start craving them even if you think you can do without them or would like to not need them. Addiction can make you disoriented and fixated on planning ways to get that drug or alcohol into your body. Addicts often make incredibly poor decisions, which can damage relationships, physical well-being and mental health. If you feel you can't cope without drugs or alcohol, get help as soon as possible. Alcoholics Anonymous is a widely regarded resource for addiction: www.aa.org. If someone in your home or your life drinks or uses drugs in a way that makes you uncomfortable or scares you, you don't have to handle it on your own. Talk to someone you can trust, or reach out to Alateen, an anonymous organization that was created to help people living with the effects of someone else's drinking (or drug use). Their website is www.al-anon.alateen.org.

THAT'S WHAT HE SAID . . .

"My worst and most life-changing experience with alcohol was in college. My brother came to visit me, and the first night he was there, we drank a lot. I got very sick from alcohol poisoning and spent the rest of the weekend very ill. To this day—25 years later—I can't even smell whiskey without getting nauseous, and I can't tolerate most alcohol at all. The decisions I made that night changed my life and my tolerance for alcohol forever."

Can Too Much Screen Time Be a Problem?

While many boys—and men—like to spend time in front of the TV or computer screen (shout out to all my gaming pals!), it has become increasingly concerning to many people how many hours we all—and especially boys—spend in front of a screen. If you find yourself avoiding responsibilities, missing homework and social deadlines and spending time with your screen so you don't have to deal with people, you may need help organizing your time and prioritizing your resources and energy. While the distractions of the world of fantasy and play are incredibly important for your development and enjoyment, they are not free of the addictive hormonal loop your brain knows so well when more time is spent with a screen than with school, social life and household responsibilities. If you think you may have a problem with the amount of time you spend watching TV or playing video games, or if someone you know is suggesting you might have a problem, learn more by talking to a trusted adult—the World Health Organization has just included "gaming disorder" in its most recent International Classification of Diseases.

THAT'S WHAT HE SAID . . .

"Computer screens offer incredibly enticing stimulus; movies, video games, social media and more. I became increasingly addicted to video games after college and struggled with that addiction for 15 years. Video games sapped my ambition for real-life advancement by satisfying that ambition with virtual advancement. I lost a lot of time and a lot of opportunities. With every

technological improvement, we are challenged to resist the desire to escape in this way, and it's not easy."

WHEN FOOD BECOMES A PROBLEM

Food is nourishing and critical for our health, and we discussed the science of nutrition as you Boy Up in Chapter One. A lot of people would not associate Boying Up with eating disorders, but as we discussed, boys and men can have eating disorders, and it is almost always because of unrealistic perceptions or expectations about their bodies. There is a lot of pressure in our culture for men and boys to have a certain body type. Being tall, having broad shoulders and a lot of muscle definition are considered ideals for many cultures, especially Western cultures. There are many boys who take the images they see in the media and compare themselves. Many men diet or work out obsessively, and some even get plastic surgery or take drugs like steroids to try to have their bodies look like the images of models and actors usually shown as attractive. Steroids are very harmful to growing bodies and can eventually affect your ability to function normally; they can even lower your sperm count, thus affecting your ability to become a dad someday. If you find yourself obsessing about a part of your body and going to great lengths to manage your diet because of the impact you fear it will have on your body, or if you spend excessive time away from family, friends and activities because you want to dedicate that time to exercising or grooming, you may want to talk to someone about the way you're feeling about your body.

SOLITUDE AND SILENCE

Something that might happen when you are upset as a boy is liking to be alone and not wanting to talk to anyone. Since my sons were about 8 years old, they have sought out solitude when mad or frustrated. Many times, they make it very clear they don't want to talk when they are upset. Sometimes they shout, "I DON'T WANT TO TALK, MAMA!"

"MESSAGE RECEIVED!" I sometimes playfully shout back! And then I let them be.

When they first started doing this, I was very concerned, because girls and women, for the most part, like to talk things out and be around people when they are upset. *How am I supposed to make my boys feel better if they won't let me talk to them and hug them?!* I thought to myself.

What I learned from friends of mine who have boys (and from the many male friends in my life whom I took this problem to) is that for many boys and men, solitude and silence help them regroup and calm down when they are feeling really agitated. Also, since many men are often not super comfortable crying or expressing their feelings in front of others, it makes sense to seek out a space to have their feelings without fear of judgment or being teased. Should boys and men be allowed to express their feelings and *not* be teased or judged? Absolutely. But since in many cultures that is not the norm, it's okay for boys and men to seek out safe places where they can feel their feelings and cry if they need to.

Alone time can actually be a very important part of learning to cope with stress, so it's important to make the most of your time spent with yourself when you need emotional support. Here are some things to do alone to cope with stress—and these are not good for just boys; girls can use them too. And I would know because these are *my* most helpful stress tools when I'm alone!

1. **Shake things up.** Any time you do something outside of your normal routine, your brain gets a wake-up call. It's like you're saying to a stressed-out brain, "Hey, there! Let's try something different!" Even small changes to your routine can be a good place to start in working on stress. Go someplace you've never gone. Walk a different way to homeroom. Explore a park you've never been to. Talk to a kid in school you've never talked to. Try a different food for lunch. Rearranging the stuff in my room was something I used to love to do; I would change the trinkets and books I had on my shelves or switch up the posters on my walls just to do something different. Any change can be good change, even small changes!

2. **Shift your perspective.** Positive thinking and "self-talk" might sound silly, but you'd be surprised by how much scientific evidence there is that it actually works to improve our mood and decrease the negative impacts of stress. Inspirational quotes can be found all over the internet, and when you find one that inspires you, copy it and post it on your mirror or inside of your locker. (Some of my favorites can be found at the end of this section.) Remind yourself if you're feeling down that life gets better. You won't always feel sad, even if you feel sad right now. Flood your brain cells with positivity; it works.

3. **Look to Nature.** The wonders of the natural world have been celebrated for all of human history. The oceans, lakes and streams; mountains, hills and valleys; the clouds and the sky and all of the wonders of the natural world have inspired poets, painters, rabbis, priests, imams and monks for as long as humans have walked this earth. Nature has a way of making us feel very small (There are so many stars in the sky and planets out there, how can I even matter?!) and also very big (This universe is so huge, and I get to be a part of it—wow!). Try to bring even small doses of nature into your day. Look at a plant or a beetle that you normally might

walk right by. Admire the way a tree arches up to the sky, seeking nourishment from the glorious giant hot ball of gas that is the sun. Follow a leaf as the wind carries it along a street. Take a second to appreciate that all of these things are not created by humans, but rather are the product of the glory of the scientific world and natural events of the universe. It should make you feel both humble and empowered, and it can have a super-positive effect on your overall mood and attitude.

4. **Move your body.** Research has shown that walking even for 15 minutes around the block can really boost your mood if you make a habit of it. Sometimes boys—and even men—will say that walking isn't "real" exercise, but they're wrong. There are more ways to increase the circulation of blood and oxygen than boxing, wrestling or running a marathon. Moving your body around by walking a few times a week gets your heart pumping and elevates your happy hormone levels, and that's what we all need!

5. **Make some art.** Making art and learning about art are great ways to expand your mind and feed your creative brain, which can boost your mood tremendously. Painting, drawing or even working with clay can be very therapeutic. My younger son

Dancing in Your Boy Body

When you think about a dancer, you usually picture a woman, right? Or a man who might get teased for being such a huge fan of dance, right? Men have always participated in dance: from ancient ritual and Native American dances to ballet, jazz, and hip-hop. Have you ever heard of Fred Astaire? The Nicholas Brothers? Mikhail Baryshnikov? Savion Glover? The movie *Billy Elliot*?! These are some of the world's most famous dancers, and they are worth checking out. These male dancers have amazing physiques, a fantastic lung capacity, and have found a wonderful creative outlet for aggression and emotion. Dancers are incredibly strong and tough. Try it for yourself—you'll see!

will draw out his feelings; everything from things going on with his and my relationship to events in worlds he creates in his mind. I like listening to music that speaks to how I'm feeling, especially when I'm down. I also like to play the piano, because it feels like my emotions get more manageable when I can play them out. My older son feels the same about his piano relationship. Sometimes I'll write in a journal about my feelings, and I sometimes write poetry because I like the challenge of finding words that rhyme to match my mood. In middle school, poetry was a really safe place for me to share my feelings for Mischa, the boy I had a big crush on but who barely knew I existed.

As a grown-up, I make collages out of pictures and cloth and fabric and anything I have around the house, because being creative is soothing, and making something out of nothing gives the brain a real boost.

6. **Learn to meditate.** Meditation is something you can do on your own any time of day or night with little or no preparation needed. A basic sitting meditation practice starts like this: sit in a chair with a straight back. You want to be comfortable, and there shouldn't be any strain on your back or neck. (You can also lie down to meditate, but the key is to not fall asleep, and when I lie down, I tend to want to go right to sleep!) Close your eyes gently and become aware of your breath. Breathe slowly and deeply and try to just focus on being aware of your breath. It's totally normal to have other thoughts come into your head, like what's for dinner or what homework you have to do or how cute so-and-so looked waiting for the bus today. Even with a lot of meditation experience, I still think about what's for dinner and the dishes that have to be cleaned and also sometimes handsome men when I meditate; trust me, it's hard not to think about other things! But there's no need to feel bad about your mind wandering. Just let the

thoughts pass on by without you beating yourself
up over not being able to focus. The goal is to not
have as many thoughts come and for them not to
stay very long. Keep in mind that people practice
their whole lives to perfect this, and monks in
some religions literally spend their entire lives
mastering meditation; it's not easy! Just like you
have to build up a muscle when you want to learn a
new sport or lift weights, meditation takes practice
and the use of the most powerful "muscle" in your
body: your brain!

7. **Enjoy simple pleasures.** There are simple things
   that make me happy when I'm feeling down or
   stressed out, like having a cup of tea or writing a
   letter or email to a friend I haven't spoken to in
   a while. Or riding my bike or taking a jog. If you
   promise not to laugh, I'll share with you one of
   my silliest but most favorite simple pleasures . . .
   I have a folder in my desk of pictures I love of cute
   animals. It's mostly monkey and cat pictures I've
   collected from magazines. I look at these pictures
   when I need a smile. I know it's silly, but it's
   something that costs no money, doesn't require
   a membership to a club and takes just a second.
   It really does work wonders for me to peek at
   a monkey wearing glasses and a top hat, and I

know that my brain is thanking me for that shot of cuteness. Simple pleasures can go a long way. It's important to find what those simple pleasures are for you.

Some Inspirational Quotes

"Faith is taking the first step, even when you don't see the whole staircase."—*Dr. Martin Luther King, Jr.*

"We tend to have more faith in what we imitate than in what we originate. We often feel that we cannot derive a sense of absolute certitude from anything which has its roots in us."—*Bruce Lee*

"Human happiness and human satisfaction must ultimately come from within oneself. It is wrong to expect some final satisfaction to come from money or from a computer."—*Dalai Lama*

"Train yourself to let go of everything you fear to lose."—*Yoda*

Meditation for Inspiration

Here are some meditations you can do on your own once you are breathing slowly and deeply. Even doing these for 5 minutes can make a big difference in how your body reacts to stress on a daily basis.

1. **Locate the breath.** Concentrate on where you feel the breath as you breathe. Focus on the breath starting in your belly, and try to feel your belly

expanding like a big balloon as it takes in air. Breathe in through your nose and feel how the air tickles the outside of your nostrils. Let the breath out through your mouth slowly and feel the air as it moves past your lips. Keep doing that, taking slow and deep breaths. The goal is to be still with the breath and not force it at all.

2. **In and out.** Try counting breaths and try to let that number be the only thing in your head. So breathe in and think, *In one,* and then when you breathe out, think, *Out one,* and then take a second deep breath and think, *In two,* and then exhale and think, *Out two,* and so on. How many breaths can you count to without losing concentration? If you get distracted, don't sweat it. Just start again and try to get to a higher number.

3. **How long can you breathe?** Slow your breathing down and take long, deep breaths without feeling like you are holding anything in. Count how long it takes to take a full breath in and then count how long it takes to breathe it all out. Usually the exhale is longer than the inhale. Can you breathe in for 5 seconds and then out for 7? Can you slow your breath down even more so that you breathe in for 6 seconds and out for 8? You shouldn't ever feel out of breath; the goal is to train

your body to slow your breath down and to quiet your thoughts while you focus on the breath.

4. **Walk!** If you want to do a walking meditation, remember that you need to keep your eyes open! Go somewhere where you can take about 10 steps in a straight line. It should be a quiet place, like a hallway where people won't be walking around, or in a yard or a park. Lift one leg and start to take a step very slowly, so slowly that you need to balance on the leg that's supporting you while you move your foot as slowly as you can. It might feel funny at first, but the idea is to move with mindfulness and intention, and to be very deliberate. When your foot hits the ground, think about the heel hitting first, and then let your foot unfold onto the ground very slowly. Don't rush into lifting the other foot right away. Feel how your body adjusts to having two feet on the ground rather than just one and then shift your body to the front foot so you can slowly begin to lift your back foot. As you lift it, think about what it feels like to be aware of the back heel coming up first, followed by the rest of the foot peeling off the ground. Lift slowly, once again balancing on the leg that's supporting you. Return to the start and breathe and feel the stability of being on both feet again. Now it's time to take

your second step! It may also help to think of these words as you do this meditation: *lift* (for while you are slowly lifting your first foot), *place* (for when you place the foot down), *shift* (for when your body shifts to the front foot), *lift* (for when the back foot comes up) and *place* (for when it comes down again).

COPING WITH STRESS WITH THE HELP OF A COMMUNITY

Although seeking some solitude is normal and may be necessary for you, keep in mind that in very stressful times and when you are experiencing prolonged stress, it's important to find ways to trust people by reaching out and not isolating yourself if you're struggling. Stress and sadness thrive in darkness, and we have to bring them out of the darkness of our brains and hearts to shed light on them.

Relying on other people for help and support is not something that comes naturally to all of us, especially men in our culture. But keep in mind that for all of human history, people have lived in communities, because it allows them to know each other and help support each other. Community means there are people around you who know you and your family, and who can be there in a way that works for you. Maybe you've experienced this in your community if there was a natural disaster such as a fire or a flood or an earthquake or a tornado. Have you noticed how people come together to help each other? And not just firefighters and the police—community members are supposed to help each other, and they often do.

Don't be afraid to share your feelings with others. If you don't feel comfortable talking to someone in your family, find a school counselor or teacher you can trust. Sometimes the parents of a friend might feel like good people to talk to, and that's a safe place to start as well.

Another way to cope with stress is by participating in events where people already congregate. Have your parents ever tried to make you go to a religious service when you're going through a rough time? It can feel awkward, and it can make you feel vulnerable, and that can be uncomfortable, but it can also help a lot. The reason it's encouraged is because it's good for us to be around people so that we don't have to go through tough stuff alone. By doing this, we start to learn more about what and who can be helpful to us.

Over thousands of years, religions have created a lot of rituals that can help in times of stress. So even if organized religion isn't something you think you want to be a part of, there are aspects that we can apply to our lives even outside of a formal religious setting, which can support our mental well-being.

Here are some of the benefits people have found from being a part of a religious community that comes together in stressful times.

1. **Help.** Have you ever been away at camp and felt homesick? Or have you ever been upset about something at school? Chances are, you got a taste

for what community can do for you when you needed it in those situations. Community helps you feel not alone. Having people around can distract you in healthy ways and help you understand your feelings in a larger context than if you tried to figure it all out on your own. In communities that are close, when someone in the family dies or when a new baby is born, people show up right away with food and help arrange for taking care of the small kids so that the adults can talk and work out details without worrying about making food and caring for children. It really helps to have people around when stressful things happen, and communities make that possible. (Of course there are nonreligious communities and activities that can make this kind of connection happen as well, but the structure of religious organizations causes people to congregate regularly and get to know each other on a more regular basis.)

2. **Focus.** Sometimes when we are stressed, it feels like the stressful thing is all we can think about. Gathering together in a peaceful setting such as a church or synagogue or mosque or temple forces us to shake up our thoughts and try something new in our brains. It forces us to focus on something other than the stressful situation. This kind of focus helps

the brain start to get on board with shifting the
stressful dynamics that are happening. The sadness
or frustration or despair or anger we may be feeling
can be disrupted—even for a short time—and this
starts a pattern in your brain of working things out.

3. **Prayer.** Prayer is a form of talking things out.
Even if you don't believe in God, you can benefit
from having quiet time to talk out—even in your
head—what's going on. Prayer can look like a lot
of different things, and it can often feel like a lot of
thanking God for stuff. This might not seem like a
logical thing to participate in if something horrible
is going on, but the process of prayer allows us to
find places in our brains and hearts where we can
be grateful for things that are okay even when there
are so many things that may not feel okay. Shifting
our thinking from "everything stinks" to "certain
things stink, but certain things don't" is a really
good start toward helping your brain get you out of
a stress funk.

4. **Meditation.** Many religious traditions incorporate
meditation into their practice, especially the
Eastern religions. If you think of prayer as talking,
meditation is just listening. There are many ways
to meditate, but the basic idea is to stop what
you're doing and find a quiet space to be with your

thoughts and to breathe slowly and deeply—kind of cool, right? And what's even cooler is that scientific research has shown that meditating improves immune system functioning and is linked to less anxiety and depression, so meditating is really a win-win choice for healthy coping! (See the box on page 157.)

GETTING HELP COPING WITH STRESS

What about other ways to help with stress? When stress makes it difficult for you to do schoolwork or causes problems in relationships with your family and friends, it can be helpful to talk to your parent or a school counselor. You may also find that talking to a professional outside of your school, who is trained to help you with your problems, is helpful, too. One of the most revolutionary thinkers the world has ever seen was an Austrian man named Sigmund Freud, who studied neurology about 150 years ago. Freud was the first person in history to describe how talking about problems out loud can lessen the weight and stress associated with them. Along with another doctor named Josef Breuer, Freud was the first to demonstrate and communicate how, when people form a relationship with someone who talks to them about their feelings and their struggles, they transfer some of their pain to that person, who can then help them work through it. This was the start of psychoanalysis, and it's the basis for what we now call psychotherapy or talk therapy, which can be helpful for men and women and boys and girls alike.

Sometimes when we are under stress, we have a lot of problems with sleep, or we may have thoughts in our heads that won't go away. For some people, this kind of stress may lead them to do certain things (actions, thoughts, breaths) repeatedly to help cope, and this can escalate and become disruptive to their lives. While psychotherapy is also helpful for this, another kind of therapy that can be used for this kind of stress is called cognitive behavioral therapy (CBT). CBT is designed as a more short-term, goal-oriented kind of therapy, where you have worksheets and "homework" to do and review with a therapist. CBT helps you understand your motivations for thinking the ways you think, while helping you find more productive ways to work through stress.

The scientific basis for talk therapy and CBT are the same: by behaving and thinking differently, we can change the chemistry of the brain so that we can make stress easier to deal with. There is no "magic" to therapy; the key is to be consistent with seeing a therapist and to ask questions when you don't agree with something or when you hear something that doesn't feel right to you. Most importantly, therapy can only work if you feel comfortable talking with the therapist. If you don't feel like you can share things with one therapist, ask to try another until you find one you can talk to openly and honestly.

A lot of therapy is not covered by insurance, and it can be expensive, but there are more and more free services popping up all over the country to allow people to talk through their problems. Sometimes it can be scary to talk about feelings, but it really can help, and even a school counselor is a good place to start, since many are trained in basic therapy techniques.

Besides therapy, you've probably heard about medications that people can take to help them deal with stress. These are usually prescribed by a psychiatrist, which is a doctor who specializes in people's emotions and the medications that affect them, but some pediatricians prescribe them, too. While these medications can indeed encourage your brain to send out more happy hormones and help decrease the sad ones, they often have strong side effects and they are not always made for growing bodies. Medication is often used when other ways to cope with stress don't work, or when someone's reactions to stress are affecting their ability to handle school, relationships and the way they function every day. It's important to know that medication doesn't have to be a forever thing. Sometimes people use medications to get through a particular situation, but with time, things get better and they find other ways to cope that make the medications not necessary. Only you and your parents and a doctor can decide what's best for your family, and often, when medication is prescribed, talk therapy can also be really helpful. In addition, it is very important to talk to your doctor or your parents when you have very unusually strong symptoms or if you have any questions about taking medication.

•, • •

Wrapping Up

In case you think I'm just making all of this coping stuff up, I'm going to share something super personal with you. You may know me from TV, or your parents may have bought you this book because they know me from TV, but I'm a real person who has lived through a lot, and a lot of it has been stressful. My family didn't have a ton of money when I was a kid, and life wasn't easy for me. In addition to shedding many tears over crushes I had that were unrequited and the death of my childhood cats when I was in middle school, which many of us experience, I was very small for my age and I developed late, so I was teased often. I cried a lot and felt left out of many things my whole life, and I still feel that way as an adult sometimes. My family had a bunch of secrets, and I felt scared a lot.

I got divorced several years ago and moved houses within the same year, which hits on two of the "most stressful things" listed at the start of this chapter. The same year, I was in a car accident that led to several major surgeries. The following year, my dad got sick and died, I went through a major, devastating breakup, and my 13-year-old cat had to be put down. That's another bunch of big stressors, right?

The things that I've talked about in this chapter that you can do to cope with stress are things I've done myself, and they are things I still do in order to maintain my emotional and mental health. They also affect my physical health, since stress impacts the body as well.

Here's what I do:

- I take walks a few times a week.
- I try to get time in nature, even if it just means hugging a tree whenever I can.
- I go to synagogue and pray that I will have patience with people and things that annoy me. I also pray that I'll have a better perspective on life when I need it.
- I practice deep breathing and try to meditate a few times a week, sitting in my bed and listening to the sounds around me, even if all I can hear is cars and my own messy thoughts.
- I force myself to be in social community settings at least once a week so that I don't isolate myself from people.
- I make lists of things to be grateful for every day, even if it's just a few things like being grateful for having clean water to drink and my cat who needs me.
- I play the piano and sing sad songs when I need to be reminded that I'm not alone; there are musicians whose lyrics indicate that they have also experienced sadness, too. Listening to music with lyrics I can relate to helps me work through hard feelings.
- I go to therapy every week and talk about my feelings, even when it's hard and I don't want to.

- And don't forget my folder of pictures of cute
  monkeys and cats . . .

All of the things I do to cope may not feel like they are work-ing right away, but with time and patience, they do help. All of the things we do on a daily basis to reduce our stress and help us cope contribute to our overall well-being and mental and physical health in the long run. From one stressed-out person to another, I hope you will trust me and find ways to cope that bring you joy and peace.

SIX

• HOW BOYS MATTER •

We have been exploring a lot of the nuts and bolts of Boying Up so far: how your body grows, how you learn, how you navigate dating and socializing, how you cope with hard stuff . . . It seems like we've kind of covered it all. But there is another very important part of Boying Up, which involves thinking about how decisions you make play into the Big Picture of your life. I suppose the question we all wonder about sometimes is: do we matter in this world? I hope you agree that we do! The decisions you make and the things you say and do can impact other people in very powerful ways. Part of the process of Boying Up and becoming a young man who is compassionate, kind and confident involves finding ways to make impacting others in a positive way a significant part of your life.

The Future

One of the ways we start to understand our potential impact and influence is to think—even for just a little bit—about the future.

And don't worry: I'm not talking about planning out the rest of your life right now. Even if we tried to, we couldn't know what was going to happen anyway! When I say we should think about the future, what I mean is this: it's not too early to start thinking about what you might want your life to look like when you are done Boying Up and have become a grown-up boy.

Why is it important to think about this kind of stuff now? Because the choices you make now actually affect what your future will look like. And no, I'm not saying that the flavor of ice cream you choose tonight will determine where you live or that that time you told your parents you turned off your phone but you really stayed up playing your favorite video game until 2 AM is going to come back and haunt you for the rest of your life. And I'm for sure not saying that skipping class last Thursday is going to negatively impact your chances of being able to own a car someday.

What I am saying is this: what you do now frames your life and your attitudes. So while chocolate or vanilla tonight may not matter, you know that what you put into your body over time does matter. And while sneaking in some video game time is fine, keeping to your word and being trustworthy is incredibly important. And last Thursday's class doesn't matter (well, unless it was the day of an important test), but consistently choosing to miss class does matter.

You don't have to plan out the rest of your life today, tomorrow or next week. But it is a great idea to think about the future, because thinking about your future and talking it out with someone else is a great start to making your future whatever you want it to be.

After High School

Finishing high school is a huge accomplishment, and whenever you achieve an accomplishment in life, the following question is bound to come up: what next?! Here's a chart that lays out different options, so you can see what some choices might be.

LIFESTYLE

One of the best exercises to do when you want to ponder the future is to think about what kind of life you see for yourself when you grow up.

For example, do you think being a husband and a dad is in your future? Once you decide to become a dad, your life changes dramatically. Being a parent is the hardest job I've ever had—and it's also the best job I've ever had. For most of human history, we have thought of childcare as the woman's job, but we have come a

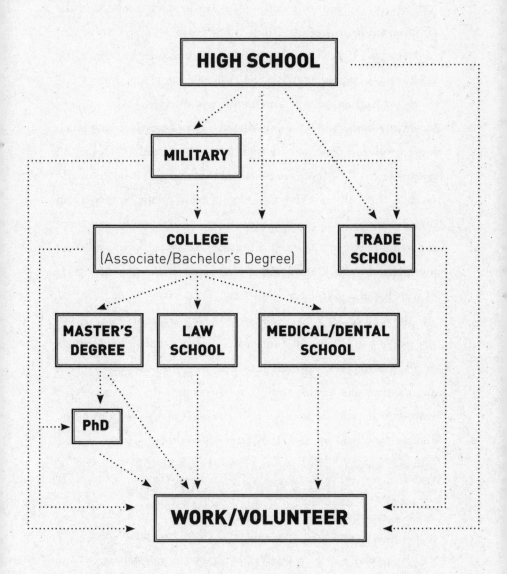

long way since men were out hunting while women tended to the children and wove baskets. Modern relationships often involve a lot of participation by the male partner, and decisions that used to be solely up to the person giving birth are now made together.

More and more men are choosing to be active dads, whether by staying home while the other partner works, or by being much more involved than men have traditionally been with childcare and housework. While there are certain things that only women can do (such as physically carrying a developing baby, giving birth to it and breastfeeding), men are important parts of any family, and there is no task they can't help with! Rocking babies to sleep, preparing food, cleaning the kitchen and folding laundry are all critical parts of your life as a partner and a parent.

Remember that once you have kids, they are yours forever, and the rest of your life pretty much revolves around planning for their needs: feeding them, clothing them, making sure they go to school and do their homework and get to soccer practice and all of the stuff your parents do for you. Being a dad is a huge responsibility, and the more you prepare, the better off you'll be.

THAT'S WHAT HE SAID . . .

"Being a father is so meaningful. One of the few things you can look at evolutionarily that is most significant is the parent-child relationship and the importance of raising kids. We are built for that role and to feel its

significance. I'm not a stranger to intense feelings, and I'm not aware of anything else that stimulates me as emotionally and intensely as being a father."

When you think about the future, where do you see yourself living? Would you like to stay in your hometown? Is being close to family an important factor in your decision about where you might live after high school? If it isn't, what are some of the places that you can imagine moving to? Could you imagine living in another country? If you can't imagine living in another place, do you want to have a career that allows for a lot of travel? If so, there are many jobs that involve traveling, such as working for a hotel or tour company, being a pilot or flight attendant, working in business consulting, or even working as a performer on cruises and at resorts. If travel is something you can picture yourself doing, know that there are ways to make that a part of your life.

Even though all of these decisions seem so far off, it's never too soon to start thinking about what you see your life looking like in just a handful of years. Letting your mind wander can sometimes be a really healthy exercise!

COLLEGE

While there are jobs you can get right out of high school such as in food service and retail or working in an office, many people choose to go to college because the degree you get when you go to college opens up a different pool of jobs, and it often sets you on a course to earn more money and have more experiences in the working world.

If you aren't ready or don't have the grades to enter a 4-year college right away, starting at a community college is a good plan to consider. You can transfer your credits from the classes you take at a 2-year college to a 4-year one when you're ready, or you can earn an associate of arts degree (also known as an AA). There are advantages to community college: it gives you some time to adjust to the workload of college in a smaller setting, and since many basic courses at community college are pretty much the same as at a larger college, you are able to save a lot of money by taking those classes closer to home. This means you can live at home and save the money you would have had to spend on renting an apartment or moving into a dorm.

In a 4-year college, there are two main degrees you can get: a bachelor of arts and a bachelor of science degree, more commonly known as a "BA" and a "BS." BA degrees are in subjects like English, history, political science or communications; these are known as the humanities. BA degrees can also be in one of the arts, such as drama, creative writing, painting, music or dance. Some people choose to get a BA degree focusing on literature in a language other than English. You can even study abroad if you want to, whether you're studying another language or not! (Think of all the pizza and pasta you could eat if you studied in Italy!) Some schools also offer a bachelor of fine arts, or BFA, which involves spending a lot of time in a studio making art or music or theater or creative writing.

Even though BA degrees are based on the humanities subjects, almost every college you can get a BA degree from also educates you in the basic math and science that you'll need for general knowledge in your life and career. Most people you encounter working in a nonmedical or nonscientific field likely have BA degrees if they went to college. So whether you choose to be a preschool teacher or a manager of a clothing store or restaurant, or if you want to work in a lawyer's office or work for a website, a BA is a great start.

BS degrees are in the sciences, such as biology, chemistry, physics, engineering and, my personal favorite, neuroscience. Many people with BS degrees go on to medical or dental school so that they can be doctors or dentists. I went to graduate school to get a PhD in neuroscience after getting my BS degree, and people with PhDs typically teach in colleges and universities and, if those degrees are in the sciences, do medical research.

MORE COLLEGE?!

Some people enter the workforce armed with their BA or BS degree after their undergraduate degree is completed. Others pursue more schooling to get a more advanced degree. People who want to get more education and a higher degree have to go to some sort of graduate school to get that degree. Graduate school is basically college after college, but with smaller, more specialized classes. And even though college after college sounds like way too much school, here are some things to know about the kinds of degrees you can get if you go to graduate school, and what you can do with them.

1. **Master's degree:** A master's degree is a degree you get with 1 or 2 more years of school after your BA or BS. It gives you more specialized knowledge about a certain topic, which you are tested on at the end of the program. Sometimes you write a big paper on your topic of study when you're done. Many people who are teachers have master's degrees in education—and other people in schools, such as social workers, guidance counselors, speech therapists and physical therapists probably have them, too.

2. **Law school:** Law school is the graduate school you go to after you get your BA or BS degree if you want to become a lawyer or a judge. Many people who work in politics obtain this degree, too. Law school is typically 3 years, and lawyers and judges work in courts, but they also do a lot in offices.

3. **PhD program:** Getting a PhD (or doctor of philosophy degree) involves doing research on

a subject that has never been done before. This research can be on pretty much any subject you can think of, and these programs take anywhere from 3 to 7 years. For my PhD, I studied obsessive-compulsive disorder, which is a disorder where people focus on certain things and have a hard time breaking out of the cycle of focusing on those things. I worked with people with developmental delays and special needs. I studied for a long time to get my degree, and I learned how to be a teacher and how to do research, and I wrote a really long paper when I was done called a dissertation—mine was over 300 pages! PhD students often go on to be professors at universities or work for companies that need the specific knowledge they have. It is very exciting and rewarding to be a part of research that can change people's lives through the discoveries you might make. And you get to be called Doctor, too, which is kind of neat!

4. **Medical school:** Medical school is the path to becoming a medical doctor, or MD. Medical school takes 4 years, and after that, you typically spend more time to get specialized training for the area of medicine you plan to practice.

5. **Dental school:** Dental school is similar to medical school in terms of how long it takes to finish, and in

the end, you have a dental degree that lets you take
care of people's teeth.

NO COLLEGE?

Some people decide not to go to college, and that is also totally
fine. If you don't go to college after high school, what can you do?
Well, some people go to trade schools to learn specific skills. Trade
schools train you to have specialized jobs—like being an electri-
cian, a plumber, a welder or even a chef. When you go to a trade
school, you can start as an apprentice until you have the skills to
work on your own. You can start earning money sooner than if you
went to college, but your job choices are going to be different.

Some people choose to join the military, often because the military pays for your education and you pay that debt back to the
country in active service or in the reserves. Other people join the
military because they feel it's their patriotic duty or because there's
a long tradition in their family of being part of the military world.
The decision to join the military is a huge one, and you should
speak to your family if you are considering such a life-changing act.
It is a brave and courageous decision to serve your country this way,
but it is not without risks. You'll need your parents' permission if
you decide to enlist before you turn 18, so make sure to open up
a conversation as soon as you can to start thinking more about the
impact it could have on you and your family.

Men Who Matter

Frederick Douglass was born a slave in Maryland around 1818. He never knew who his father was, but it was likely the owner of the plantation where he was a slave. He was separated from his mother as a young child and

FREDERICK DOUGLASS

IT IS EASIER TO BUILD STRONG CHILDREN THAN TO REPAIR BROKEN MEN.

was taught to read and write by the wife of the slave owner he was sent to serve. He escaped from slavery after several failed attempts and went on to be one of the primary leaders of the abolitionist movement, helping to single-handedly change the perception white people had of African Americans and change the way slaves saw themselves. Douglass was a gifted speaker and held several public offices. He wrote many autobiographies detailing his life as a slave and then as a free man. He is known as the most influential African American of the 19th century.

The Reverend Dr. Martin Luther King, Jr., was an American Baptist minister and activist who was the most important leader of the civil rights movement of the 1950s and 1960s. He used nonviolent

MARTIN LUTHER KING, JR.

LOVE IS THE ONLY FORCE CAPABLE OF TRANSFORMING AN ENEMY INTO A FRIEND.

protest to gain rights for black people based on the model of Indian leader Mahatma Gandhi. Dr. King devoted his life to speaking, protesting and leading a movement that transformed the landscape of America and the world. His "I Have a Dream" speech is one of the most important in modern times, as it calls on Americans to dream of a time when no one will be judged by the color of their skin but rather by the content of their character. He received the Nobel Peace Prize in 1964 and was tragically assassinated in 1968.

The Dalai Lama is the 14th leader to hold that title. He was born with the name Lhamo Thondup in 1935 in Tibet, a country that is part of China but is a separate entity. He is a

DALAI LAMA

monk, which is the name for the religious leaders of Tibetan Buddhism. He took on political duties as the leader of the people of Tibet when he was only 15 years old, just after China made Tibet part of its country. When he was 24, political fighting in Tibet forced him to flee to India, where he lives as a refugee. He travels the world giving speeches about the rights of his people, science, women's rights and human rights. He uses his religious and spiritual knowledge to teach people how religions can better get along together. The Dalai Lama is a wise and generous man known for his patience, open-mindedness and kindness.

Steven Spielberg was born into an Orthodox Jewish family in 1946 in Ohio. He had a strong interest in filmmaking and made his first movie at age 16. He went on to direct and produce some of the most celebrated movies in Hollywood, such as *Raiders of the Lost Ark*, *The Color Purple*, *Empire of the Sun*, *Jaws*, *E.T.* and *Jurassic Park*. He also made a film about the Holocaust called *Schindler's List*. Besides the movies he has produced, directed and won so many awards for, Spielberg does a great deal of charity work, such as establishing the Shoah Foundation, which archives the stories of people who survived the Holocaust.

STEVEN SPIELBERG

Neil deGrasse Tyson is an astrophysicist, author and science communicator. He is the director of the Hayden Planetarium in New York City and is one of the most famous and beloved scientists many people have ever known about! He was raised in the Bronx in New

NEIL deGRASSE TYSON

York, and he became consumed with his love of physics from an early age. He has written books, hosted countless television shows about science and has made so many people interested in science who never would be interested before. He is known for his charisma and his great sense of humor as well as for providing answers to some of the greatest mysteries of the universe.

Fred Rogers was a puppeteer and host of a TV show from 1968 to 2001. *Mister Rogers' Neighborhood* entertained and educated decades of young people. Inspired by the desire to transform TV into something that could help people, Mister Rogers hosted

FRED ROGERS

a show aimed at preschoolers, which taught ethics, morals and creative appreciation for the world through puppets, songs and storytelling. Also trained as a Presbyterian minister, Rogers was an inspirational artist and personality who touched the lives of hundreds of thousands of people in his lifetime.

Causes

One of the most important ways to start imagining how your life will look and how you can make your life matter for you and those you love is to consider what you're passionate about. Finding a cause that is important to you helps you learn more about the world around you. Your brain needs a lot of information to form opinions, and the more you learn, the better you can know what you think and how to be a part of changing things in this world.

What matters to you? Are there things you hear on the news that bother you? Maybe it's a story discussing racism or gun violence, or maybe news reports on the damage that is being done to the environment or to certain populations in the world. Maybe it's a story about how an animal was found in the street after it had been mistreated by its owners.

There are things going on right in your neighborhood that probably need your help. If you live in a city, there might be concerns about how the homeless population is treated. There is litter in most every city or town that needs to be dealt with. There are beaches that need cleaning up, parks that need repair and dozens of other ways we need to make changes that will better things for everyone.

If you ever look at the problems in your community and our world and think it's just such a mess that it can never be fixed, guess what? You're wrong! There are lots of things we can do to make changes to this world, and every small gesture of loving kindness and care helps. You're not too young to find ways you can give back to your community, your city, your country or even the world.

Even if a change is small, it can still be a big deal. Here are some examples of charity projects that have been started by kids not much older than you—and in some cases, maybe younger.

1. **Alex's Lemonade Stand Foundation.**
   Alexandra "Alex" Scott was not even one year old when she was diagnosed with neuroblastoma, a type of cancer. When she was 4 years old, she held her first cancer fundraiser in her front yard and raised over $2,000. Tragically, she died when she was 8, but in her precious short life, she raised over $1 million for research into cures for childhood cancer. Her family has continued her legacy by continuing her mission, and Alex's Lemonade Stand has now raised more than $150 million for cancer research and support for children with cancer and their families.

2. **FundAField.** When soccer fans Kyle and Garrett Weiss were 13 and 15 years old, the brothers traveled with their family to see Iran play Angola in the FIFA World Cup. It was Angola's first ever time in the World Cup, and Kyle and Garrett were shocked to see that the Angola fan section was so small. They came to learn that impoverished countries have very little funding and support for soccer and that the luxuries they

took for granted—such as cleats that fit—were
not something every child could have. This was
the start of a large and now successful campaign to
build soccer fields, provide soccer equipment and
encourage support for African children to have the
resources to learn and enjoy soccer.

3. **Positive Impact for Kids.** When she was 12,
   Leanne Joyce was at a cardiology checkup for a
   heart condition, and she was touched by a gift she
   was given by two teenagers who were hospital
   volunteers. Their act of kindness made her commit
   to giving back, and she formed an organization that
   helps fulfill the wish lists of hospitalized children
   in North Carolina and beyond. Over $130,000
   has been raised, and that money is used to change
   children's lives in hospitals.

4. **Love in the Mirror.** When Jonas Corona and his
   brother, Maximus, were 4 and 2 years old, they
   went with their mom to volunteer in Skid Row,
   a part of Los Angeles that is populated by a lot of
   homeless people. He saw many adults and especially
   children without proper clothing. At the age of
   6, Jonas decided he wanted to help everyone have
   clothing that fit and felt good so that they would not
   feel like they didn't fit in when they looked in the
   mirror. So he started his own organization to collect

things like clothing, toiletries and even food to help
the homeless. To date, over 45,000 people have
received these basic necessities, and the organization
has grown to include toy drives and the donation of
school supplies for homeless children.

Although these organizations don't fix the entire problem of pediatric cancer or give basic necessities to the millions of homeless people all over the world who still need them, these are examples of small and significant projects that have a tremendous impact on people.

You don't have to solve the whole problem at hand in order to matter. You don't have to fix the world; you just have to start with what you can do with your resources and build from there. Every time you touch a person with kindness, the world gets a little bit brighter. And you never know how your kindness will affect someone else. It might cause a ripple effect so that your gesture makes them want to do something about a problem, too—that's often how this works.

You get to do your part and see how good it makes you feel to support a cause you believe in and to watch the positive effects you can help bring about. If establishing an organization or raising money sounds like too much to start with, here are some examples of small actions that can have a big impact:

1. **Donate what you don't need.** Go through
   your closets and drawers and all of the closets

and drawers in your house (with your parents'
permission!) and find things you are not using
anymore or that don't fit. You can donate
used toys and clothes and really anything in
fair condition to a local charity. Charities that
run thrift stores sell items and use part of the
profits to support the charity and the people
who work there. There are also places to
donate used clothing to homeless shelters in
most major cities.

2. **Hold a clothing or food drive.** Any
time you have the opportunity to interact
with a group of people, such as at school or
in after-school activities or community or
religious activities, you have the opportunity
to get a larger group of people to become
involved in a charity project. When I was 15,
I started a canned-food drive at the TV studio
where I was filming. I posted signs all over
and walked around handing out flyers on my
lunch break to anyone I could. My first year, I
ended up raising an entire van full of canned
goods for a homeless shelter. People loved
the opportunity to contribute, and it felt
especially good to be a part of something as a
group. The more, the merrier!

3. **Collect spare change for a year.** Do you
   ever find loose change on the ground? Or have
   you ever put on a pair of pants you haven't worn
   in a while to find $1 or even $5 in the pocket
   that you had forgotten was there? I collect spare
   change and "found money" like that in a jar, and
   at the end of 12 months, I see how much is in
   there and donate it. Sometimes I pick a charity
   to send the money to, and sometimes I use
   that money to buy a sandwich and a drink for a
   homeless person sitting outside of a restaurant or
   store I'm going into. It's a small thing to do, but
   it does make a difference in someone's day, even
   in a small way.

4. **Pick up trash.** Whenever I go to a park or
   to the beach, I see trash everywhere, and you
   probably do, too. The next time you see trash,
   don't ignore it; pick it up and throw it out! Bring
   a plastic bag with you to the beach or the park
   or on a hike and collect trash. You can even use
   plastic bags as "gloves" if you come across messy
   or sticky candy-bar wrappers and stuff like that.
   If everyone picked up a handful of trash, we
   wouldn't have so much trash lying around! It
   feels good to be a part of the solution and not
   the problem, and even though some places need

a whole lot more cleanup than a few pieces of
trash here and there, all you have to believe is
that every little bit counts—because it does.

Volunteering

A terrific way to make a difference in others' lives is to take your
passion for something and volunteer your time and energy toward
it in a meaningful way. When you make a choice to volunteer for
a cause you believe in, you are setting aside time to participate
in working with an organization or group of people who want to
make change in practical ways. In my life, I have volunteered to
pack goodie boxes for soldiers overseas during the holidays, and I
have helped answer phones and do office duties for organizations
who could not afford to pay people to do that work. My favorite
volunteer position when I was a teenager was working in a senior
citizens' center.

How did that come about? Well, if you have any elderly people
in your family or close circle of family friends, you might already
know that spending time with someone who has seen a lot more
of life than you have is a terrific way to learn about the world and
how fast it's changing and will continue to change. I grew up with
grandparents with very heavy accents who were immigrants from
Eastern Europe. They left war-torn countries against all odds for
the safety and security of America, working long hours in unsafe

conditions to make money to support themselves and their families. They grew up in a world without computers or cell phones—can you imagine that?

I think you can get so much from being around seniors. So I literally walked into the office of a senior citizens' center in Hollywood when I was 17 and asked if I could volunteer there. The job I was given was to serve lunch to about 50 senior citizens every weekend.

The time I spent getting to know the people at this center was incredibly valuable. I made friends there, and I learned about how everyone came to Hollywood: some grew up there, and many of the people I served lunch to came to this country from other places: Cuba, Armenia, the Philippines. It was a real experience getting to hear about their lives. Many of them did not have much family, and I was sometimes the only person who wanted to talk to them. It made me feel good to be of service to them, and I could tell from their smiles and hugs that it made them feel good, too. A lot of my new friends spoke very slowly, and it helped me practice being patient and kind even if I had somewhere to go and things to do. I learned skills for preparing and serving food, and I found a source of compassion for these kind people that has stayed with me my whole life.

Volunteering gets you into the world of others and gives you the opportunity to make a difference in someone's life today.

• • •

THAT'S WHAT HE SAID . . .

"Volunteering reminds me that I am part of something greater than myself. Connecting to something that is bigger than me is a reflection of my commitment to engage with the Divine—because that is bigger than me! Volunteering is also about giving back by expressing gratitude for what I've been given and what I've accomplished and worked for in my relationships and my life choices, including the gifts I receive from mentors and loved ones. Being of service allows me to be a conduit to what others are seeking, whether in a contract, a career, transforming a community by helping them obtain water rights or equal treatment for LGBTI individuals, or singing a song or prayer that connects them to something greater than themselves."

Wrapping Up

There is a lot of pressure in our culture for men to be a lot of different things at once. Men are told to be strong—but not too strong; to be sensitive—but not too sensitive; to work hard—but not too hard; to play hard—but not too hard. It can be confusing to figure out how exactly to be and what matters most.

I certainly don't have the answers for every boy and man,

but here's what I tell my sons: Boying Up doesn't end when you become a legal adult; it's a journey that stays with you for the rest of your life, because it's about laying the foundation for a life of healthy and satisfying decisions. There are many ways you can make your life matter.

For some boys, becoming a man will be about forming friendships with guys that will be the basis for a lot of interactions. Meeting girls or boys they're attracted to and dating them may also be a big part of some boys' journey. Sports may be a huge part of your Boying Up. For other boys, drawing and listening to music and learning how to play instruments will be part of the process. For still others, becoming a man may be a difficult time full of uncertainty and a lot of feeling like you don't fit in with most guys. This might be because you like things many guys aren't interested in or because you have special needs that make a lot of seemingly simple interactions complicated, or it could be that you're just not into a lot of our culture's expectations for boys and men. All of these pathways are legitimate, and they are all okay.

Whether you become a stay-at-home dad or the president of the United States, there are ways you can make an impact on the people around you and the world around you. It starts by believing you matter and by seeing your journey as one of many steps linking together to form the pathway to the rest of your adventure as a young man.

• AFTERTHOUGHTS •

When I was given the green light to write *Boying Up*, I was thrilled and excited—for a few seconds. Then I completely panicked. How would I write this book!? While I am trained as a neuroscientist and spent 12 years of my life in school to get my degrees, my knowledge of the brain, nervous system and endocrine system seemed suddenly insufficient when I thought about the real-life nuts-and-bolts process by which boys become men.

As the mother of two sons—one of whom is entering the tween phase—I was reminded again and again as I wrote this book that, despite my degrees, helping my boys navigate this journey isn't an easy task. Our culture's expectations of what that journey should look like has long been insufficient to encompass all of the kinds of journeys boys will go on as they Boy Up. Especially now, when our society is recognizing the power inherent in being a boy and urging boys to use that power for good—to speak out for what's right and help to empower girls and young women—things can feel even more complicated. This Boying Up stuff is hard!

Boying Up is a journey I can only observe from where I stand:

as a scientist, as a mom and as a part of a culture that often gives conflicting directions about how to Boy Up. The challenges are myriad, and I don't have all of the answers. What I hope you have seen in these pages is the kind of analysis I have chosen to participate in so that I can best support my boys as they enter manhood—and best support you, too, so that you grow into smart, thoughtful, bold, brave and brilliant men. I hope this book is a conversation starter for anyone who is a boy, was a boy or is helping love a boy into manhood.

Thank you for coming along on this journey with me.

• ACKNOWLEDGMENTS •

I first and foremost thank my wonderful and endlessly optimistic editor, Jill Santopolo, for helping me bring my perspective to the community of *Boying Up*. Jill, *Girling Up* changed my life and touched so many people; you gave me the confidence to bring *Boying Up* to life despite my fears. Thank you for inspiring me to write on. Thank you to Talia Benamy in Jill's office for bearing the brunt of the dirty work for *Boying Up*. Your voice and your dedication is so appreciated!

Thank you again to my insightful book agent, Anthony Mattero (Foundry Media); to my incredibly hardworking manager and partner-in-crime, Tiffany Kuzon (Primary Wave); and to her fearless assistant, Brandon Bonilla. And thank you to Annett Wolf and Allie Jenkins at Wolf-Kasteler Publicity for being a new part of my life as we embark on this journey together, and to Heather Weiss Besignano at Icon Publicity for getting me here.

Thank you to my mentor, friend, lawyer and one of the contributors to "That's What He Said," Shep Rosenman. Shep: you are the most giving person I have ever met. Thank you for letting me come to your house pretty much every weekend to learn how to be more like you.

And to Fulton Management and Eric Fulton: thank you for fixing my life by giving me Elizabeth Ricin and Kenny Locsmandi. I am completely inappropriately smitten with them and I am pretty certain Elizabeth and I will run away from all of you someday to live in the South of France and do puzzles all day. So . . . sorry not sorry.

Most of the behind-the-scenes mess of my life is handled by the exceptional brain of Caroline Hayes, who is as intelligent and creative as she is organized. I am so sorry if I break your brain some days, but you keep up with me so well and I am so grateful to have you as a creative partner and executive assistant.

Thank you to our copy editor, Ana Deboo; to neuroscientist Dr. Lisa Aziz-Zadeh, gynecologist Dr. Jessica Brown, registered dietician Rachel Goodman and pediatrician Dr. Lisa Nowell, who reviewed the pieces of *Girling Up* that ended up in this book in different forms; and school psychologist Dr. Samantha Winokur, who reviewed both *Girling Up* and *Boying Up*. Thank you as well to Dr. Daniel Lowenstein, the pediatric neurologist who reviewed *Boying Up* from a medical perspective and as a grown-up boy.

I have been so impressed with everyone at Penguin and I am particularly grateful to publisher Michael Green; Ellice Lee, who designed the book's interior; and our book-jacket designers, Lindsey Andrews and Maria Fazio, who came up with such a playful and awesome cover. Thank you also to the marketing and PR teams at Penguin who helped *Girling Up* go far and who I know will do the same for *Boying Up*!

Kenton Hoppas's illustrations really make *Boying Up* feel authentic, and he took the time to show boys in all shapes, sizes and colors, which is so important. Thank you for your artistry, Kenton!

As I crafted this book, my GrokUniverse and GrokNation team members helped me write and think and be better. To founding editor Esther Kustanowitz, and to Mia Taylor and Melissa Gruenfeld: thank you for building this world with me. And to Avital Norman-Nathman, Ramie Smith, Christina Kelly, Dalene Rovenstine and Natalie Koch: thank you for coming on board and joining the fun/chaos!

Thank you to the cast, staff and crew of *The Big Bang Theory*, who put up with my constant state of distraction all of the time, but especially as I wrote *Boying Up*. I love my job because of you all.

Thank you to my mother, who will probably never understand why God gave her such a boyish daughter. Ma: I can't help it if Dad's (z"l) X chromosome was basically made to clone him. You did good, though. And I throw "like a boy," so I suppose I turned out all right.

Thank you to my uncles, Loren Bialik, David Goldstein, Chaim Fischer and Elliot Goldstein, for modeling compassion, sensitivity and wisdom. You have been such wonderful men for me to learn from and love. And to my boy cousins who I grew up with, Seth and Jacob Goldstein: thank you for tolerating me pushing you around on the basketball court and in the yard. I didn't really mean it. (And Rebekah and I did our fair share of choreographing gymnastics routines to entertain you, so it all worked out!)

Thank you to the men I consider my brothers for helping me understand men and boys and myself in the process. Jacob Gisis (on the weekends and days ok my friend): you have been a rock for me and such a terrific playmate, and thank you to Vera for putting up with us singing, laughing and making a ruckus in her life for twenty years. And to Gabe "Uncle Gino" Chasnoff: the safety and playfulness we share is a great blessing. Thank you.

To the mystically awesome Eric Kaplan and the impossibly perfect Matthue Roth: thank you for continuing to teach me all of the mysteries of life.

Thank you to the "That's What He Said" contributors: Daniel Inlender (most reliable human ever), Chad Jamian (bringer of daily joy) and Noey Jacobson (more than just a pretty face).

Huge shout-out and unwanted emojis to Captain Ahab of Florida, the most deserving porcupine, knower of the mysteries of man, Lumberjeff Kerr McGivney, for countless appropriate distractions as I started this book (and a few inappropriate ones as well). Thank you, Jeff, for ongoing inspiration as a fellow writer, wandering spirit and philosopher of life.

To Immanuel Shalev, who I cannot live without and never want to: your faith in me is everything. *A groysn dank.*

The brave and exhausted (because of me) women who power the Mayim machine are Dr. Nancy Vanderheide and Shawn Crane, without whom I would not have the spiritual or psychological brainpower to do anything. I know I'm a lot of work; thank you for not giving up on me. Please don't.

Thank you to the Y chromosome magic of my boys, Michael Stone, for teaching me so much about the process of *Boying Up* through your stories, your journey, Jeff's journey (z"l), and the journey you take every day at home with our two miracles. Those precious *neshamas* are so lucky you are their dada. And thank you to the XX and XY who raised you to be such a Renaissance man, Sherrie Stone and Robert Stone—I love how your boy and boyish genes are now part of our family legacy.

And to Robert Anthony Mathes: thank you for helping me give birth to this book. You contributed to every chapter one way or another: with your edits, with your "That's What He Said" contributions, with your shaving tips and with your heart. Thank you for being the man you are and for not letting the sweet boy inside you go away; I love you both.

And last but certainly not least: to Miles and Frederick. You guys are so insanely awesome and I am so sorry for all of the times I embarrass you and kiss you in public or try to hold your hand when I forget you don't want to anymore. I am sorry I work so much. I am sorry I am not your stay-at-home mom, but I also know that you are sensitive, expressive, creative, thoughtful, generous, funny little men because of everything we all do to care for you. You are my rogue and my monk, my FirstBorn and my Little Man; you are my greatest blessings and you are my harshest critics. You teach me every day how flawed I am and I love you for that. May you meet only the kind of people who support your journey, and may they see in you the light I see every time I look into your faces. I thank God for you every day and I thank you every day for bringing me closer to all that is Divine. I love you, *boychiks.*

MAYIM BIALIK is best known as Amy Farrah Fowler on America's #1 comedy, *The Big Bang Theory*, a role for which she has received four Emmy nominations and a Critics' Choice Award. She also starred in the early-1990s sitcom *Blossom*. Mayim earned a BS from UCLA in Neuroscience and Hebrew and Jewish studies, and went on to earn a PhD from UCLA in Neuroscience. She is the author of *Beyond the Sling*, *Mayim's Vegan Table* and *Girling Up: How to Be Strong, Smart and Spectacular*.

Mayim founded GrokNation.com in 2015 as a platform for sharing her writing on everything from religious observance to women's issues to politics to maintaining modesty in Hollywood. She seeks to present herself as a normal, imperfect mom trying to make everything run smoothly in a world that often feels out of her control. Mayim lives in Los Angeles with her strong, smart, spectacular sons.

You can visit Mayim Bialik at
GrokNation.com
and follow her on Twitter and Instagram
@MissMayim

Watch her videos at
youtube.com/mayimbialik

· INDEX ·

NOTE: Page numbers in *italics* indicate illustrations.